Sea Creatures

Illustrated by
Robin Lee Makowski

Copyright © 2006 Kidsbooks LLC
www.kidsbooks.com

Manufactured in China

0306-1C

Visit us at **www.kidsbooks.com**

INTRODUCTION

This book will teach you how to draw many different types of sea creatures. Some are more difficult to draw than others, but if you follow along, step by step, then (most important!) practice on your own, you soon will be able to draw these fascinating animals. You also will learn methods for drawing anything you want by breaking it down into basic shapes.

One basic and commonly used shape is the oval. There are many variations of ovals: some are small and almost round, others are long and narrow, and many are in between.

Many of the creatures in this book begin with some kind of oval. Then other shapes and lines are added to form the basic animal outline. Most times, free-form shapes are used, like the ones pictured below.

Simple lines, plus variations of other basic shapes—such as circles, squares, rectangles, and triangles—are used to connect the beginning shapes. Keep looking for these basic shapes as your work on your drawing.

Some basic oval and free-form shapes:

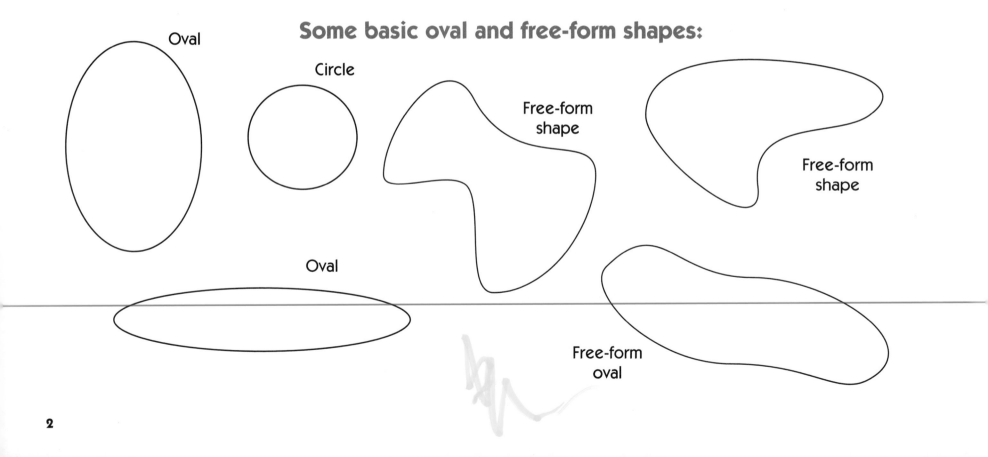

Oval

Circle

Free-form shape

Free-form shape

Oval

Free-form oval

SUPPLIES

NUMBER-2 PENCILS   FELT-TIP PEN
SOFT ERASER   COLORED PENCILS
DRAWING PAD   MARKERS OR CRAYONS

HELPFUL HINTS

1. **Take your time with steps 1 and 2.** Following the first steps carefully will make the rest easier. The first two steps create a solid foundation of the figure, much like the foundation a builder constructs before building the rest of the house. Next comes the fun part—creating a smooth, clean outline drawing of the sea creature, then adding all the finishing touches, such as details, shading, and color.

2. **Always keep your pencil lines light and soft.** This will make the guidelines easier to erase when you no longer need them.

3. **Don't be afraid to erase.** It usually takes a lot of sketching and erasing before you will be satisfied with the way your drawing looks.

4. **Add details, shading, and all the finishing touches** only *after* you have blended and refined all the shapes and your figure is complete.

5. **Remember:** Practice makes perfect. Don't be discouraged if you don't get the hang of it right away. Just keep drawing, erasing, and redrawing until you do.

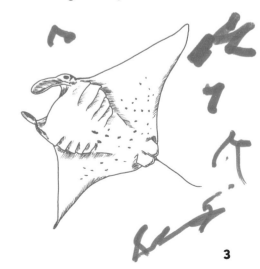

HOW TO START

Look at the drawing of the fish below. Study it. Then look at the steps it took to get to the final drawing. Note how shapes overlap and where they intersect.

Step 1. Draw the basic overlapping oval shapes.

Step 2. Add the additional shapes over the figure you created in step 1. These are the basic guidelines that form the body and create the foundation of your drawing.

Step 3. Blend and refine the shapes into a smooth outline of the fish. Add facial features and other details.

Step 4. Add scales and fin lines. Now you are ready for the finishing touches. Add shading *(see page 5)*, or color your drawing with colored pencils, markers, or crayons.

Remember: It is not important to get it perfect. It *is* important for you to be happy with your work!

Erasing Tips

● Once you have completed the line drawing, erase your guidelines. Then proceed to shading and/or coloring your drawing.

● Using a permanent, fine-line marker over your pencil guidelines will make it easier to erase the pencil lines.

● A very soft or kneaded eraser will erase the pencil lines without smudging the drawing or ripping the paper.

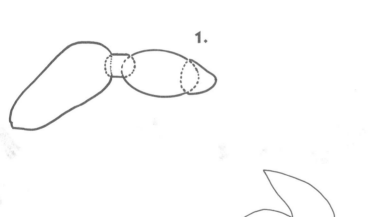
1.

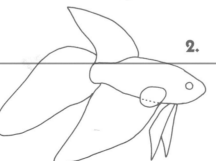
2.

3.

4.

MADE IN THE SHADE

One of the ways to add a realistic touch to your drawings is to add shading. When light strikes an object, parts of the object create shadows. Shading will help your drawings look more three-dimensional.

There are many ways to create shadows. If you are using colored pencils or crayons, simply use a darker shade of the same color on bellies, fins, or anywhere light would be blocked by the shape of the animal. If you are using a black pencil or fine-line marker, you can use crosshatching and/or stippling to create shading.

Crosshatching is making parallel and/or intersecting lines through the areas to be shaded. A light area of shade would have light, thin lines with more space between them; darker shading would show thicker, closer lines and more intersecting (crossing) lines.

Stippling is using dots to indicate shading. Tiny dots with spaces between them are used for lighter shading, while heavier dots that may touch each other are used for darker areas.

Stippling and crosshatching can be used together. Either method can also be used to indicate tone, such as dark stripes on a white animal. Practice and more practice, plus lots of patience, is needed when you are learning to use stippling and crosshatching.

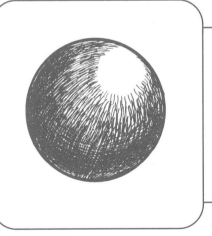

With the same light shining on these two objects, notice how circles can be transformed into three-dimensional globes by using lines (crosshatching) and dots (stippling). With crosshatching, notice how the lines follow the curve of the object. Straight-across lines would make the object look flat.

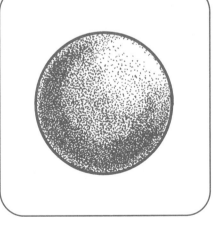

Crosshatching

Stippling

PARTS OF A FISH

The illustration below shows a fish, labeled with the names of the basic parts of a fish's body. Throughout this book, we will refer to some of these body parts.

Most of the sea creatures in this book are fish, or relatives of fish. Whales and dolphins are mammals, not fish, but some of their body parts have the same names.

1. Dorsal (back) area
2. Head
3. Eye
4. Dorsal spine
5. Dorsal fin
6. Fin rays
7. Second dorsal fin
8. Nostril
9. Mouth
10. Teeth
11. Lower jaw
12. Gill plates or gills
13. Ventral fins; also called pelvic fins
14. Pectoral (pec) fins
15. Lateral line
16. Anal fin
17. Tail stalk; also called peduncle (PEE-dun-kul)
18. Tail; also called tail fins
19. Ventral (underside) area

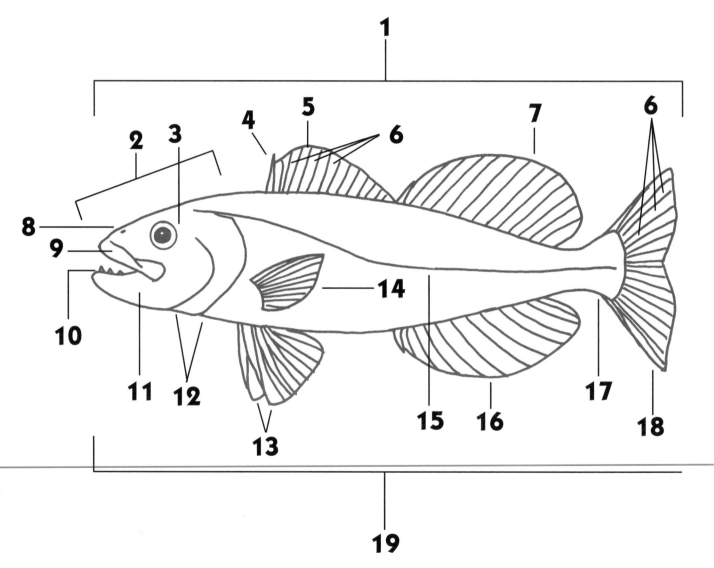

Lesser Electric Ray

If touched, the 15-inch lesser electric ray can deliver a mild electric shock, about enough to light up a 50-watt lightbulb. Found from North Carolina to Argentina, this ray is tan with smoky-brown fins and markings. This relative of the shark is best avoided!

2. Form and smooth the body, erasing any overlapping lines. Then add the irregular-shaped spots all over the body and tail.

1. Draw a free-form oval for the body, then connect it to the triangular tail by drawing a long, thin tail stalk. Draw the dorsal and anal fins, and two ovals for the eyes.

Tip: It usually is easier to draw the largest shape first.

3. Add details and shading for the finishing touches. Make the edges of the spots dark, and the centers a little lighter. Leave a white edge around the ray as you add the shading.

Orca

The distinctive black and white orca (also known as a killer whale) is the largest member of the dolphin family. Most orcas spend their entire lives in the family group, or pod, into which they were born. Each pod has its own dialect, or "accent," which members use to communicate with each other. Playful, acrobatic orcas are found in all oceans, though they prefer colder waters.

Tip: Always draw the guidelines lightly in steps 1 and 2. That will make them easier to erase later, when you no longer need them.

1. Begin with a large oval for the body, two smaller ovals for the pectoral fins, a gumdrop shape for the head, and a cone shape for the tail stalk. Add triangles for the tall dorsal fin and tail flukes.

2. Complete the smooth body outline by connecting the shapes and erasing the guidelines you no longer need. Add the notch in the flukes, and a mouth line.

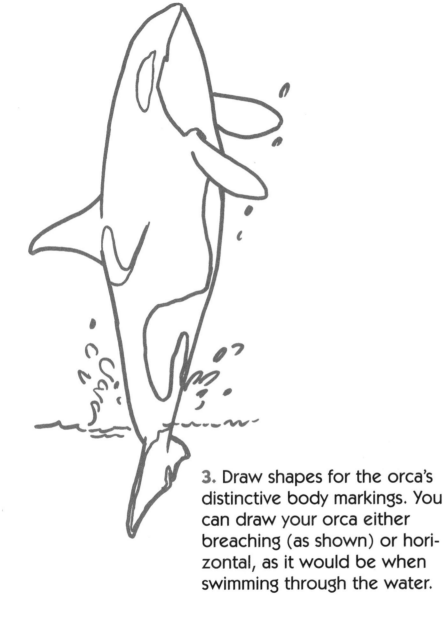

3. Draw shapes for the orca's distinctive body markings. You can draw your orca either breaching (as shown) or horizontal, as it would be when swimming through the water.

4. Complete the drawing by adding crosshatched shading. You can stipple in the gray saddle patch behind the dorsal fin. Can you see the eye between the front of the eye patch and the mouth line? When you are finished, why not draw a pod of differently sized orcas swimming together?

Great Barracuda

Growing to six feet in length, the shiny, silver great barracuda lives in warm seas. Boasting an impressive set of teeth, these barracuda are awesome predators in their reef habitats. As scary as they look, they usually are not a threat to humans.

1. Begin by lightly drawing a long, surfboard-shaped oval. Add triangles for the tail and fins. Draw the mouth with a line, and the eye with a circle.

2. Draw the gill plates and shape the fins. Note that the lower jaw is longer than the upper.

10

3. Add the markings around the mouth, the lateral line, and the body spots. Make the trailing edges of the fins ragged. Don't forget the sharp teeth!

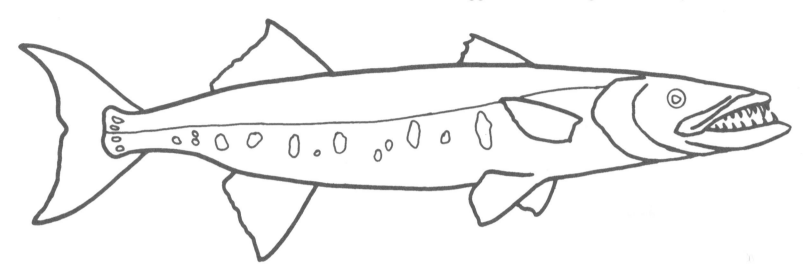

4. Add all the details and shading. Draw the fin rays—notice the white tips on some of the fins. Finally, fill in the black spots on the body. Now your barracuda is ready to hunt for prey.

Queen Angelfish

A large, tropical reef fish, the queen angelfish lives in the warm waters of the Atlantic from Florida through the Caribbean Sea to Brazil. It is dark blue with a yellow face, scales, and fins, and colorful fin tips. It grows to 18 inches in length.

Tip: Dotted lines indicate guide-lines that you will erase later, when you no longer need them.

Connect

Add

Connect

Add

1. Draw two overlapping guideline circles for the body. Add the smaller circle for the head and gill area, and a tiny circle on the front of the head. Attach the basic tail shape.

2. Connect and blend the two large circles into a smooth angelfish body shape. Erase all the overlapping lines as you go along. Add the fins, eye, and lines for the gills.

3. Add the pupil, the lateral line, and the spikes on the gill. Add the crown markings on top of the head, which give the fish its name. Now you are ready to add the finishing touches.

4. Add details, such as fin rays, scales, and shading. If you are coloring your drawing, the scales are yellow half-moon shapes on a blue background. The face, tail, pectoral fins, and pelvic fins are bright yellow. The pointed top and bottom fins are blue blending into rainbow colors at the tip, and are outlined in neon blue.

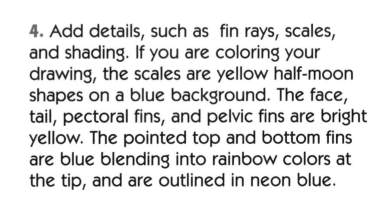

Blue Shark

Common in colder Pacific waters, the blue shark can grow to be 12 feet long. Its coloration—blue-gray above and white below—helps hide it from both prey and predators in its deep-ocean habitat.

1. Start with a long torpedo-shaped oval for this shark's body. Add the triangular dorsal, pec, anal, and tail fins.

2. Draw the mouth, eye, and the other pectoral fin. Begin shaping all the fins.

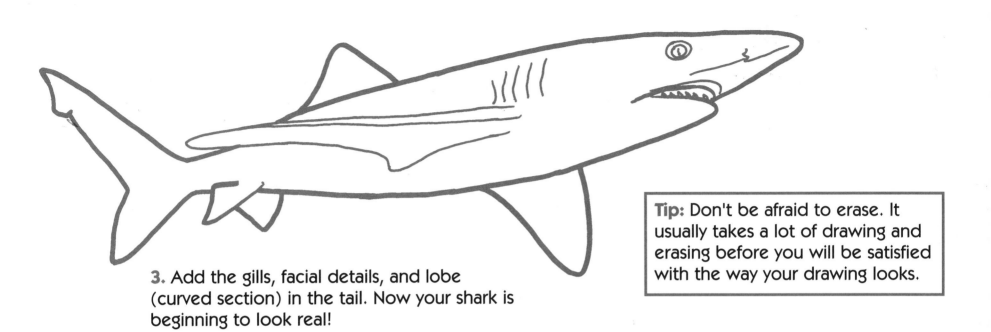

3. Add the gills, facial details, and lobe (curved section) in the tail. Now your shark is beginning to look real!

Tip: Don't be afraid to erase. It usually takes a lot of drawing and erasing before you will be satisfied with the way your drawing looks.

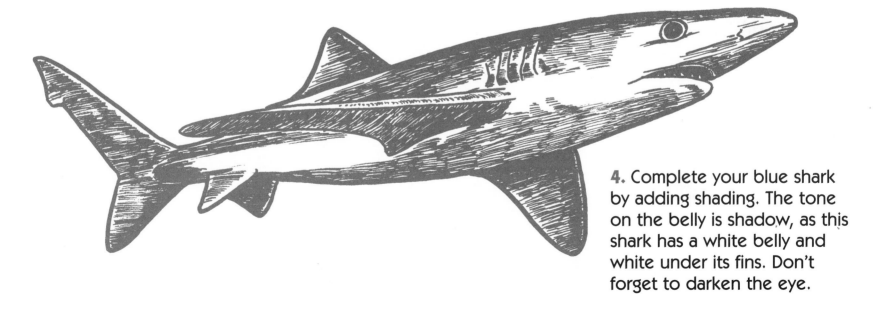

4. Complete your blue shark by adding shading. The tone on the belly is shadow, as this shark has a white belly and white under its fins. Don't forget to darken the eye.

Clownfish

The four-inch-long orange-and-white clownfish lives in a home that would be very dangerous for most fish. It lives among the stinging tentacles of the sea anemone, which anchors itself to tropical reefs. Clownfish are not affected by the anemone's poisonous sting. In exchange for a safe home, clownfish attract prey to the anemone.

Remember: Keep your pencil lines light and soft.

1. First draw a fat, baseball-bat shape for the clownfish's body. Then add the gill, mouth, eye, and fin shapes, as shown.

2. Draw the face details. (Note how the gill plate is the outer edge of one of the white stripes that mark the clownfish.) Outline the other body markings as shown.

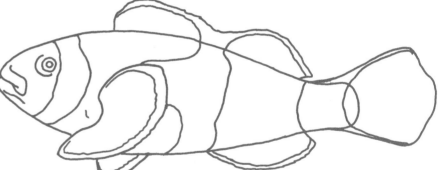

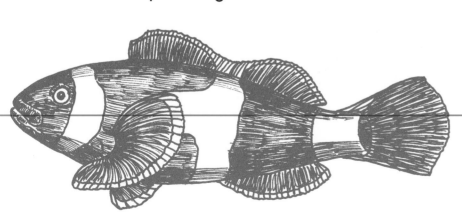

3. Draw the fin rays. You can add other details to the clownfish or color it, keeping the white tips on the fins. Try to draw several clownfish swimming in different directions.

Elephant Seal

A male *elephant seal*, called a bull, is an impressive sight! Named for its long nose, the elephant seal can rear up to fight other males with its canine teeth. This shiny, reddish-tan giant can grow to 18 feet in length. Elephant seals are found in temperate to polar oceans and spend the entire year, except for breeding time, at sea.

Tip: It is important to build a good foundation before refining your drawing.

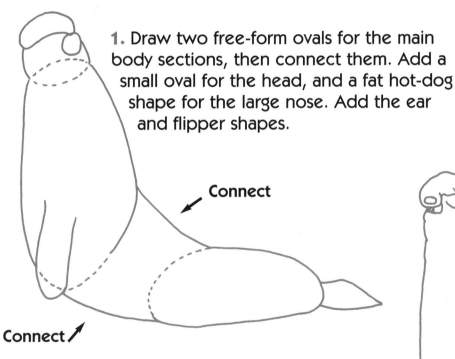

1. Draw two free-form ovals for the main body sections, then connect them. Add a small oval for the head, and a fat hot-dog shape for the large nose. Add the ear and flipper shapes.

Connect

Connect

2. Blend the shapes as you erase over-lapping lines. Add the wrinkles at the curve of the back. Draw the eye, large nose, mouth, and teeth. Then start adding details to the flippers.

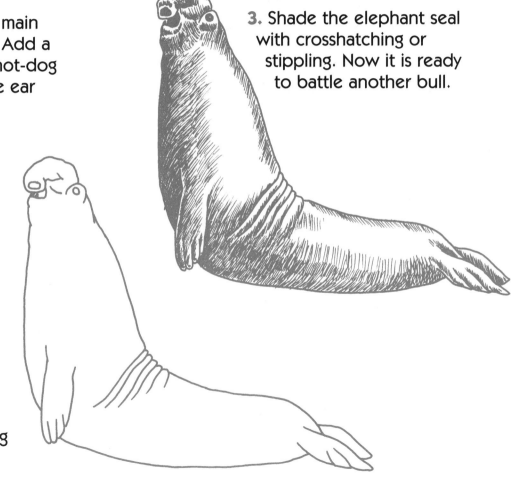

3. Shade the elephant seal with crosshatching or stippling. Now it is ready to battle another bull.

Gafftopsail Catfish

Named for the long spines on its dorsal and pectoral fins, this catfish can grow to three feet or slightly longer. Its pointy, sharp spines can cause painful wounds to humans. This fish's dorsal area (back) is blue-gray, fading to silvery sides and a white ventral area (belly).

1. Draw a long, missile-shaped oval for the body. Attach a smaller oval for the head, and create the *V*-shaped tail. (Note that the upper part of the tail fin is longer than the lower part.)

2. Connect the shapes and erase overlapping lines. Draw the large, triangular dorsal fin and the other fins as shown. Then add the guideline shapes for the gills.

3. Using light strokes, draw the eye, the long barbels (whiskers), and the spikes from the dorsal and pectoral fins. Draw the lateral line and begin shaping the fins.

Note: Make sure that you are satisfied with the way your step 3 drawing looks before going on to step 4.

4. Draw the fin rays and add details and shading. The gafftopsail catfish is a sociable fish that lives in large groups, so why not draw a school of them?

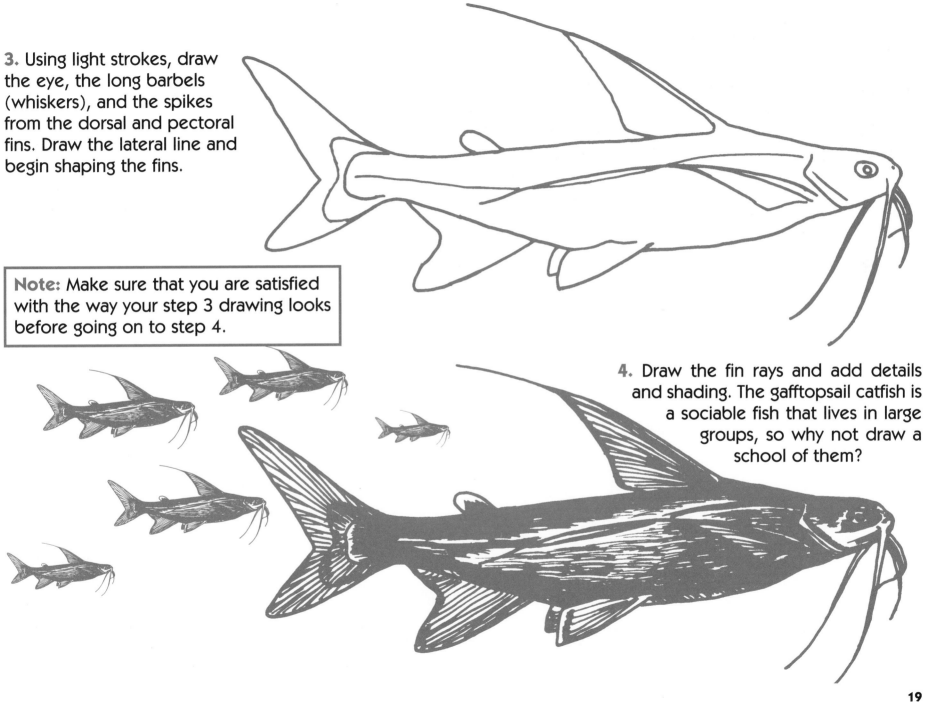

Blue Whale

The blue whale is the largest animal to inhabit Earth. It can be found in most temperate and polar seas, growing to more than 100 feet in length and weighing up to 150 tons. Blue whales are slate blue above and lighter below, with large, long spots and blotches covering the back and sides.

> **Remember:** Keep your guidelines lightly drawn.

1. Begin with a huge, pointed free-form shape, about four times longer than it is wide. At the right end, draw a long, flat triangle for the flukes.

Indent slightly

2. Draw the eye, then the mouth, dipping the curve of the mouth downward. Add the pectoral fin in line with the eye and mouth. Draw the tiny dorsal fin and begin shaping the flukes. Slightly indent the top of the head. (That is where the blowholes are.)

3. Draw the ridge and "splash guard" in front of the blowholes. Add the grooves from beneath the eye to the underside of the whale. The grooves go under and behind the pectoral fin.

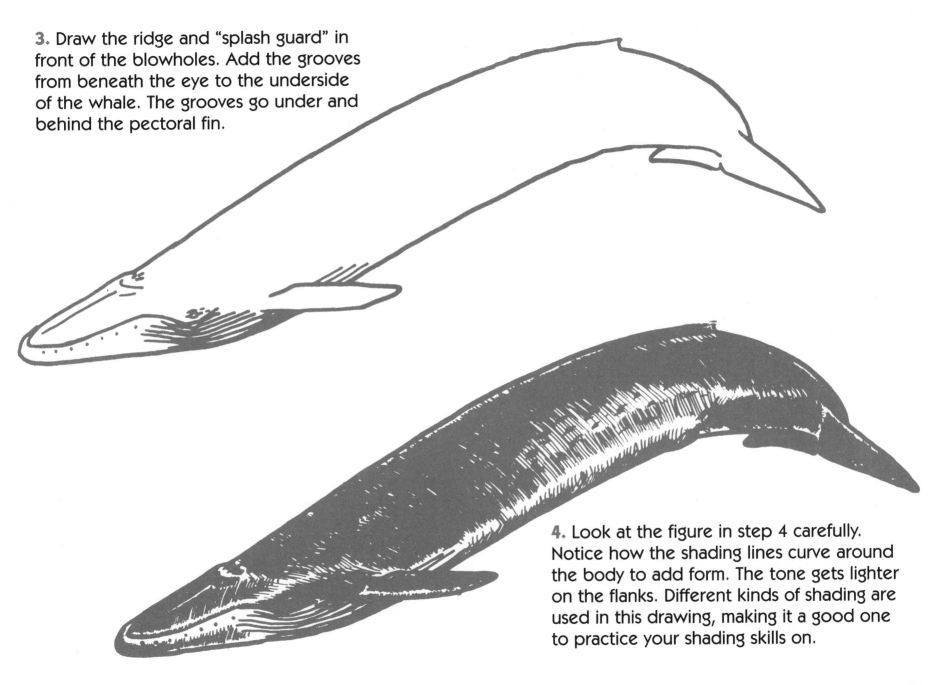

4. Look at the figure in step 4 carefully. Notice how the shading lines curve around the body to add form. The tone gets lighter on the flanks. Different kinds of shading are used in this drawing, making it a good one to practice your shading skills on.

Peacock Flounder

A strange thing happens to a flounder as it matures. Its right eye moves over to the left side of its head, so that the fish can lie flat on the bottom of the ocean and watch for prey. Able to camouflage itself by changing colors, the peacock flounder not only finds protection in its reef home, but "hides" in the open from prey. Peacock flounders grow to 18 inches in length and have blue ring markings and dots.

Stalk

1. Begin with a large oval for the body. Add a smaller oval within for the head, and ovals for the eye and tail. A spiky pectoral fin sticks up as the fish lays on its side.

2. Draw a stalk with the partially visible other eye. Add lightly drawn guidelines for the gill plate, mouth, and ventral fin. Note that the ventral fin goes across the entire bottom of the fish, and has a pointed section under the chin.

3. Sketch and blend all the shapes, erasing unneeded lines as you go along. Add the ringed markings and details to the face.

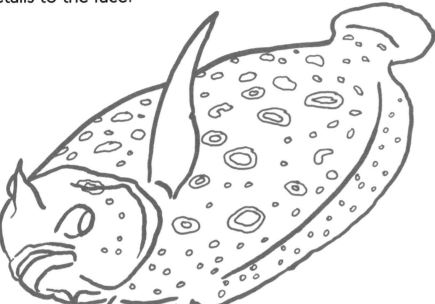

> **Tip:** Practice makes perfect. Don't be discouraged if you can't get the hang of it right away. Just keep drawing and erasing until you do.

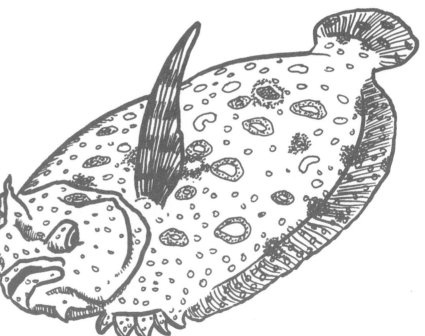

4. Draw the fin rays and all other details to the peacock flounder. Then draw a sandy sea bottom for it to lie on.

Bottlenose Dolphin

Growing to 13 feet in length, the playful bottlenose dolphin is found in all temperate and tropical oceans. Though the dolphin's body is gray above, the light belly often blushes pink when it gets angry or excited.

Tip: Take your time doing steps one and two. If you get the foundation right, the rest of your drawing will be easy to do.

1. Begin with a large, lightly drawn oval guideline for the body. Add an egg shape for the head, and a long, free-form shape for the tail stalk. Triangles of different sizes form the snout, tail flukes, and dorsal fin.

2. Smooth and combine the body shapes while erasing overlapping guide-lines. Form the flukes, the rostrum (beak), and the trademark "smile." Add the pectoral fins.

3. Add the eye just above and behind the corner of the mouth. Erase and redraw guidelines to shape the dorsal and pectoral fins.

4. Now add the texture. Curve some of your crosshatch shading lines to make the body appear three-dimensional. Shading gives your drawing a realistic look. It may be hard to get this right at first, but if you keep working at it, you will be pleased with the final results.

Deep-sea Anglerfish

Living deep in the ocean where light never penetrates, the deep-sea anglerfish is undetectable except for the lighted lure on its head. The lure attracts prey toward the anglerfish's transparent teeth.

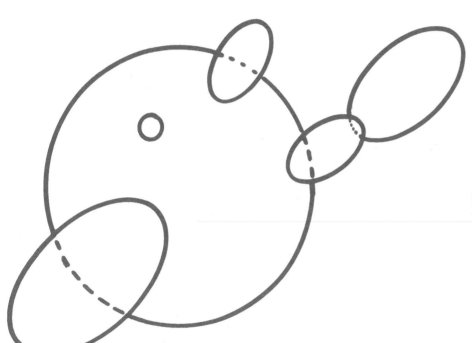

1. Lightly draw a large circle for the body of the anglerfish. Add an oval guideline shape for the lower jaw and mouth cavity. Add additional ovals for the pectoral and tail fins, and a small circle for the eye.

2. Connect the jaw oval to the body, then erase and redraw to shape the open mouth. Add the lure where a nose would be. Connect the tail stalk and tail fin to the body, and define the pectoral fin. Erase unneeded guidelines as you blend the shapes into a smooth body outline. Then draw the outline shape of the dorsal fins.

3. Draw the sharp, jagged teeth. Make the first few dorsal fins spiky, and the outlines of the other fins jagged. Then start adding details as you continue to smooth and refine the anglerfish's outline shape.

Tip: Don't be afraid to erase. It usually takes a lot of drawing and erasing before you will be satisfied with the way your drawing looks.

4. Detail the anglerfish by following the contour of its body with your shading lines. Draw the fin rays. For the finishing touch, leave the pupil bright and the teeth transparent (do this by making the inside of the mouth dark). Now your anglerfish is ready for some dinner.

Emperor Penguin

Emperor penguins live only in Antarctica. This bird has black and white feathers, and orange and yellow highlights around the head. The four-foot-tall emperor is the largest of all penguins.

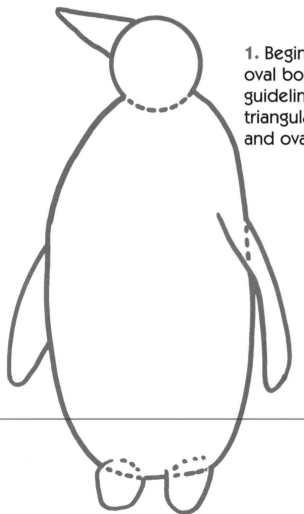

1. Begin with a large, free-form oval body shape. Add the other guideline shapes: round head, triangular beak, elongated flippers, and oval legs.

Tip: Steps 1 and 2 are very important. They establish the overall structure and look of your drawing. In steps 3 and 4 you are simply refining and adding details to the figure you have created.

2. Blend the shapes and combine them into a smooth outline of the penguin. Erase the overlapping guidelines. Draw the feet, tail, and eye, then shape the beak.

28

3. Draw the outlines of the areas to be colored. Detail the three large toes on each foot.

4. Blacken the dark areas and indicate the yellow and orange tone with stippling. The black eye is on a black background and can barely be seen. Be creative with your skills to make the eye visible. Add a mountainous Antarctica background, or have your penguin standing on an ice floe.

Flying Fish

To escape predators, the Atlantic flying fish pumps its tail and clears the surface of the water. With its pectoral wings spread wide, this eight-inch-long fish takes to the air and can glide for hundreds of feet at a time. With a blue-green back, silver sides, and golden fins, the flying fish is as beautiful as it is unique.

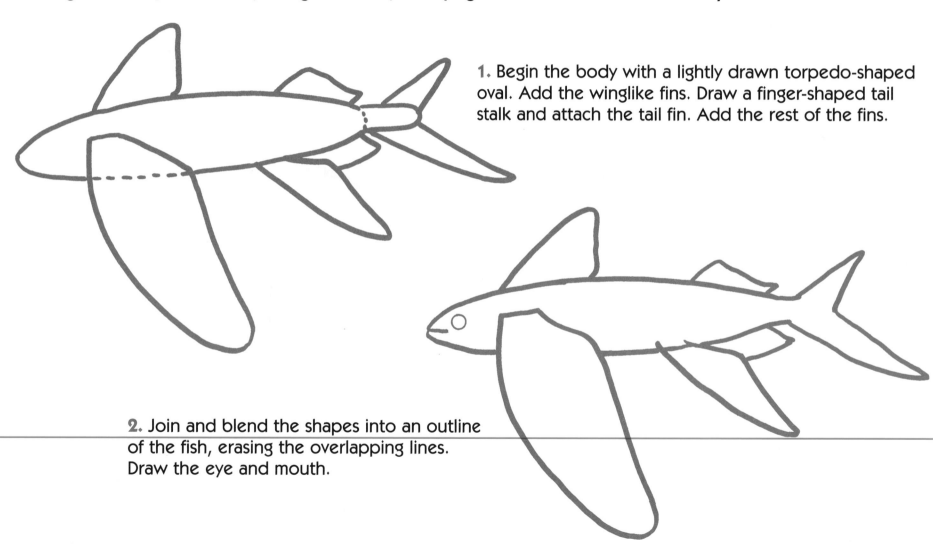

1. Begin the body with a lightly drawn torpedo-shaped oval. Add the winglike fins. Draw a finger-shaped tail stalk and attach the tail fin. Add the rest of the fins.

2. Join and blend the shapes into an outline of the fish, erasing the overlapping lines. Draw the eye and mouth.

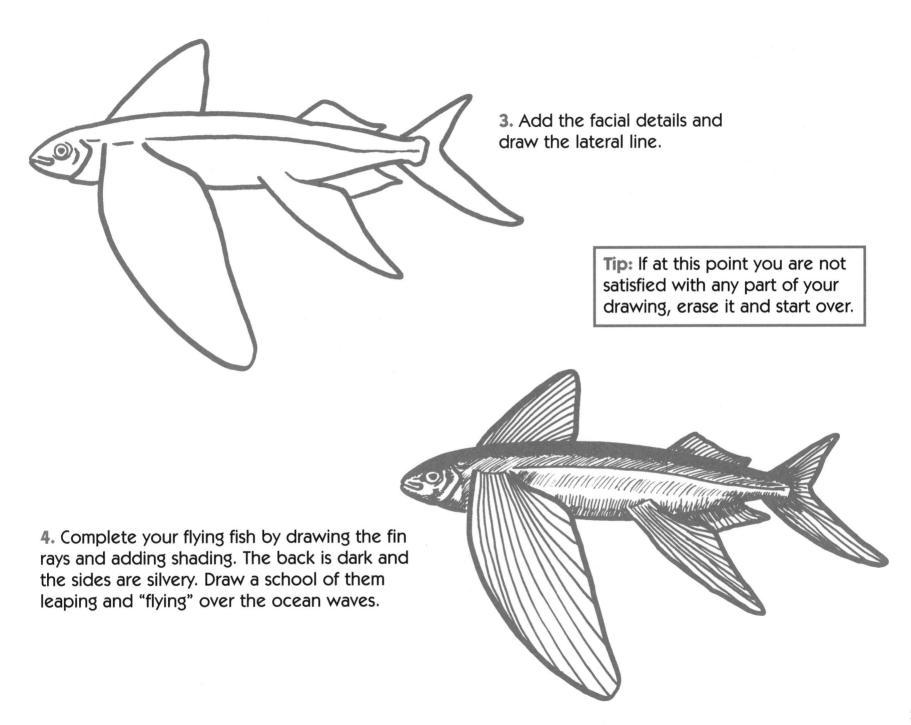

3. Add the facial details and draw the lateral line.

> **Tip:** If at this point you are not satisfied with any part of your drawing, erase it and start over.

4. Complete your flying fish by drawing the fin rays and adding shading. The back is dark and the sides are silvery. Draw a school of them leaping and "flying" over the ocean waves.

Manatee

Growing to a length of 14 feet, the gentle manatee is at home in both seawater and freshwater. One of the most endangered species on Earth, it lives in the warm springs, rivers, lakes, and bays around Florida. It must stay in water above 72°F year round or it will freeze to death. This mammal feeds exclusively on water plants, such as the water hyacinth.

Tip: Always draw your guidelines lightly in steps 1 and 2. It will be easier to erase them later.

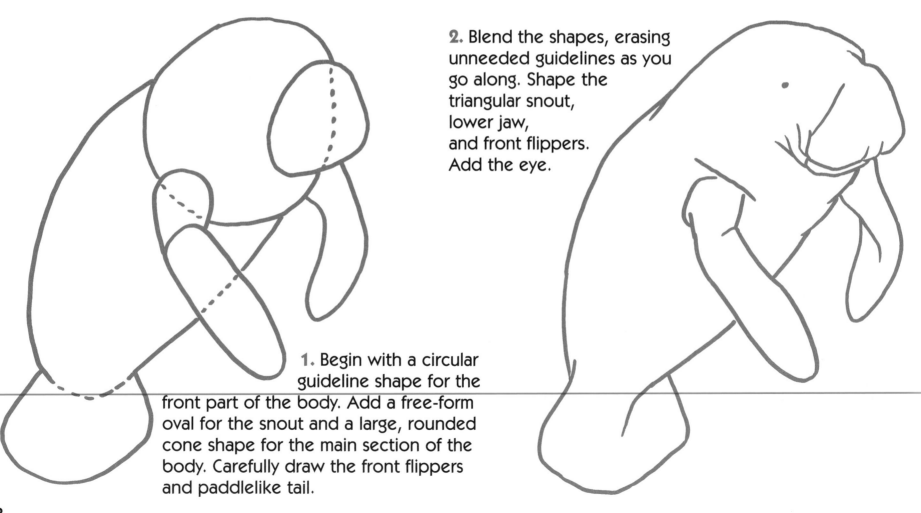

2. Blend the shapes, erasing unneeded guidelines as you go along. Shape the triangular snout, lower jaw, and front flippers. Add the eye.

1. Begin with a circular guideline shape for the front part of the body. Add a free-form oval for the snout and a large, rounded cone shape for the main section of the body. Carefully draw the front flippers and paddlelike tail.

3. Draw the rest of the face and body wrinkles, and add the nostrils. Start adding details as you continue to erase and refine your drawing.

4. Simple crosshatching will make your manatee look real. Follow the direction of the lines in the shadows. Notice the white areas which give the manatee the appearance of swimming near the surface of a crystal clear river in Florida.

Great White Shark

Great white sharks can grow over 20 feet in length, but reports of larger ones are numerous. It is probably the most well-known and feared predator. The shark has five rows of sharp, serrated triangular teeth. When a front tooth breaks off, the tooth behind it pops up to take its place, and a new one grows at the back of the row. Great whites are light to medium gray above, and white below.

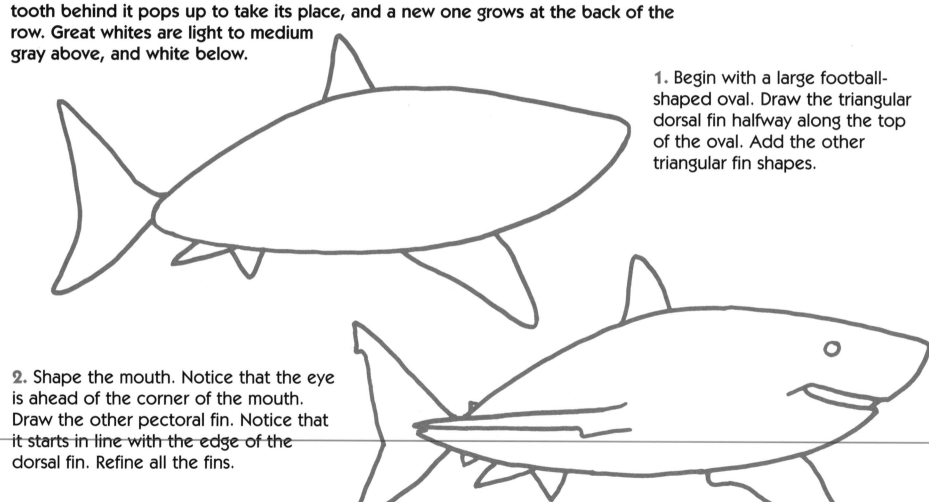

1. Begin with a large football-shaped oval. Draw the triangular dorsal fin halfway along the top of the oval. Add the other triangular fin shapes.

2. Shape the mouth. Notice that the eye is ahead of the corner of the mouth. Draw the other pectoral fin. Notice that it starts in line with the edge of the dorsal fin. Refine all the fins.

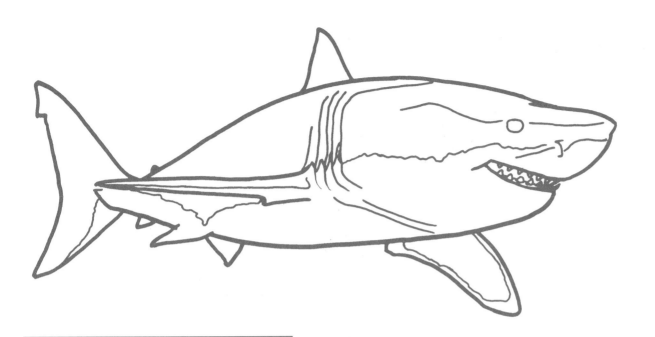

3. Draw the nose opening and the sharp, triangular teeth. Notice that the gum tissue is visible only on the bottom jaw. Draw the five gill slits right under the dorsal fin, with the last one over the front edge of the pectoral fin. Lightly indicate the lines where the coloration markings will go.

Remember: It is easy to draw almost anything if you first build a good foundation.

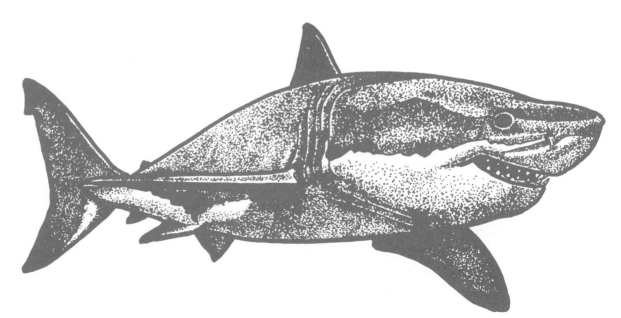

4. Complete the great white with stippled shading. Notice that even the white under the chin is stippled, to indicate shadow. You also can draw crosshatching or color your shark, if you wish.

Hawksbill Sea Turtle

This endangered marine reptile can reach a length of three feet. The sea turtle spends its entire life at sea, with the females coming on land only to lay their eggs in the sand. The hawksbill sea turtle has a dark, patterned top shell and a yellow bottom shell. The scales on its flippers and head are reddish brown above and yellow-white below.

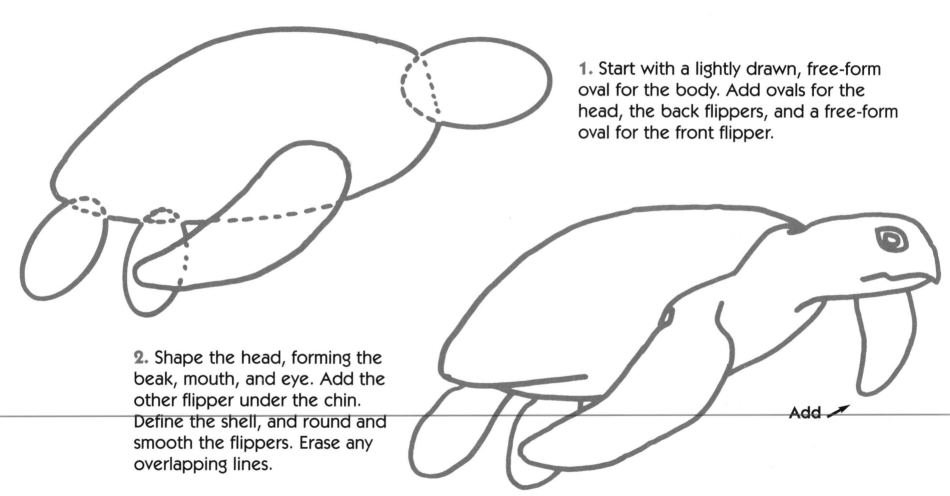

1. Start with a lightly drawn, free-form oval for the body. Add ovals for the head, the back flippers, and a free-form oval for the front flipper.

2. Shape the head, forming the beak, mouth, and eye. Add the other flipper under the chin. Define the shell, and round and smooth the flippers. Erase any overlapping lines.

Add ↗

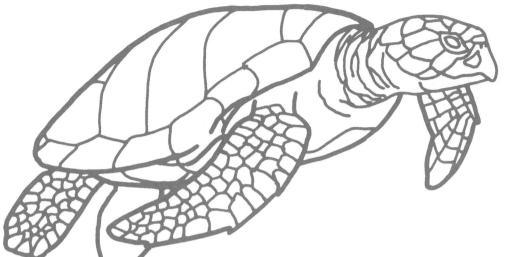

3. Draw the scales on the shell, head, and flippers. Leave the left, back flipper unscaled, as it will be completely in shadow. Draw the wrinkles on the neck.

Tips: For realistic-looking scales:
a. Draw the flipper scales in light, soft pencil.
b. Outline the flipper (not the scales) with your permanent, fine-line marker.
c. Color or marker the inside of the scales up to the pencil lines. Do not marker or color over the pencil lines.
d. Gently erase the pencil lines. The scales will remain and look naturally outlined. This trick works for fish scales and feathers, too!

4. Add the detailed shading. It looks complicated, but this animal is one of the easiest to draw realistically.

Tiger Grouper

The three-and-a-half-foot tiger grouper gets its name from its creamy-colored background and rust-colored stripes. It can go through several color phases during its life. Even the shapes of its markings can change. This reef fish lives in temperate and tropical oceans.

Tip: Studying the step 4 drawing before you start will help you understand how the basic shapes relate to each other.

1. Begin by drawing a long, narrow-ended oval. A curved triangle forms the tail, and various ovals form the fins.

2. Smooth the outline, erasing the overlapping lines. Create the head and facial features by drawing the gills and mouth. Add the eyes and nostril. Shape the fins and add the dorsal fin. (The first and second dorsal fins are joined.)

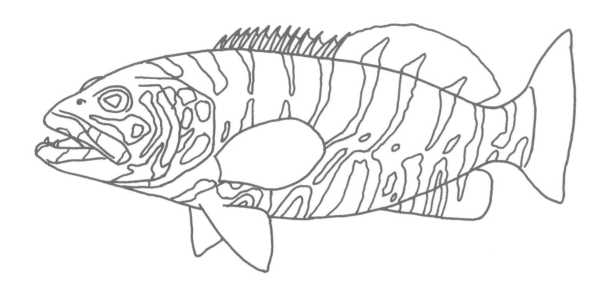

3. Draw the facial details, teeth, and the spikes on the first dorsal fin. Add the markings for the tigerlike stripes.

4. Draw the fin rays and darken the markings. Pay attention to which markings get darkened—it can get tricky! A few short horizontal lines through the light parts of the top and bottom markings will give your fish dimension. The tiger grouper is a perfect fish to add to a coral reef scene.

Hatchetfish

The deep-sea hatchetfish is equipped with a set of lights and a glowing eye to help it through its dark habitat. The lights are powered by chemical reactions , called bioluminescence *(bye-oh-loo-muh-NESS-unts)*, in the hatchetfish's body.

1. Draw a large circle for the body and a smaller one for the eye. Add a small half-oval to start the mouth, and a finger shape for the tail stalk.

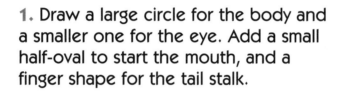

2. Shape the body as shown, erasing overlapping lines. Carefully create the open mouth. Then add the spiky pectoral, dorsal, and tail fins.

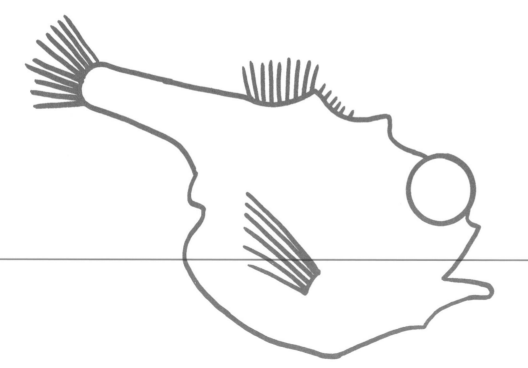

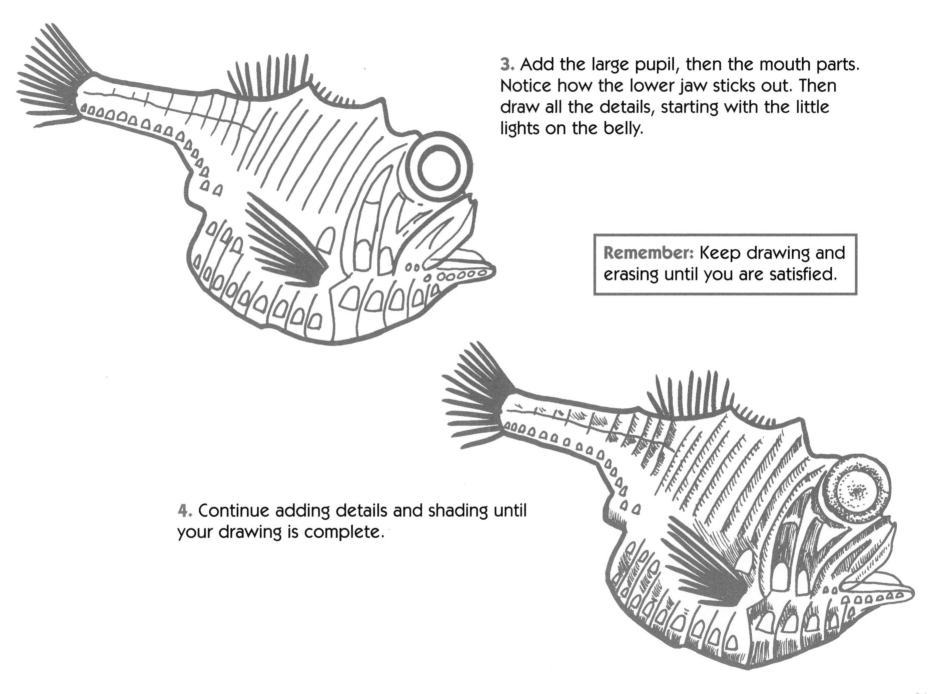

3. Add the large pupil, then the mouth parts. Notice how the lower jaw sticks out. Then draw all the details, starting with the little lights on the belly.

Remember: Keep drawing and erasing until you are satisfied.

4. Continue adding details and shading until your drawing is complete.

Horseshoe Crab

The horseshoe crab is a relative of the spider. This crab can grow to 20 inches and lives in shallow, Atlantic coastal waters. It has a brownish-gray shell and a long, spiked tail. Horseshoe crabs often gather in huge numbers on beaches during breeding season.

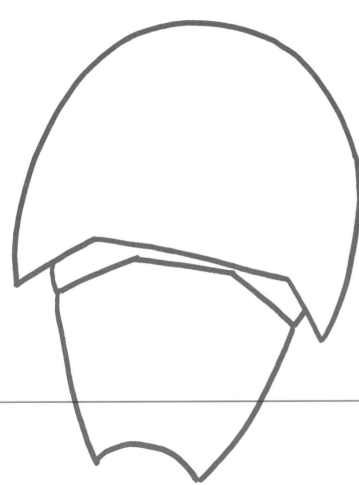

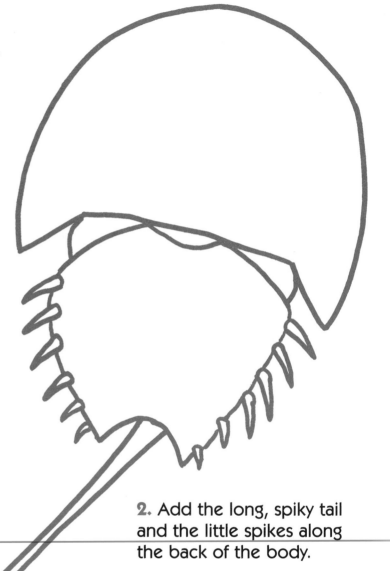

1. Begin with the largest section first—a half-oval with spiked ends, as shown. Add a cone-shaped rear section, with a crescent "bite" taken out of the back end.

2. Add the long, spiky tail and the little spikes along the back of the body.

42

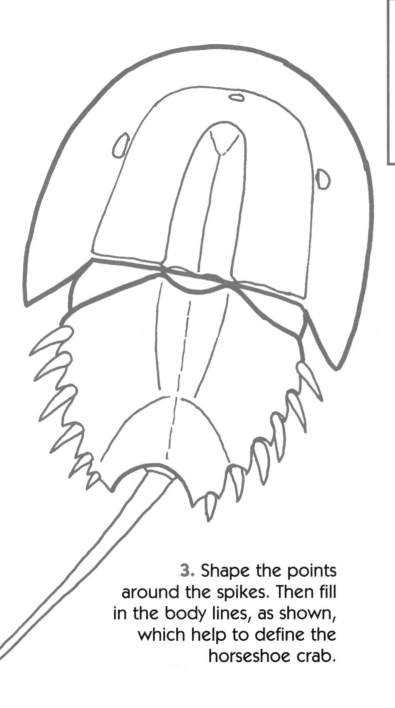

Tip: Add details and finishing touches only *after* your figure is complete and you are satisfied with it.

3. Shape the points around the spikes. Then fill in the body lines, as shown, which help to define the horseshoe crab.

4. Add shading or color to complete your drawing. If you add shading, note how the lines do not extend to the outer rim of the shell. This gives the horseshoe crab a rounded, three-dimensional look.

Blue Marlin

A billfish, such as the 15-foot blue marlin, uses its long spear to slash at prey before swallowing it. Normally, this beautiful fish is a shiny, deep blue along its back, with 15 pale blue stripes running down its silvery sides. But when angry or excited, the blue marlin's colors turn to neon, a situation known as "lit up."

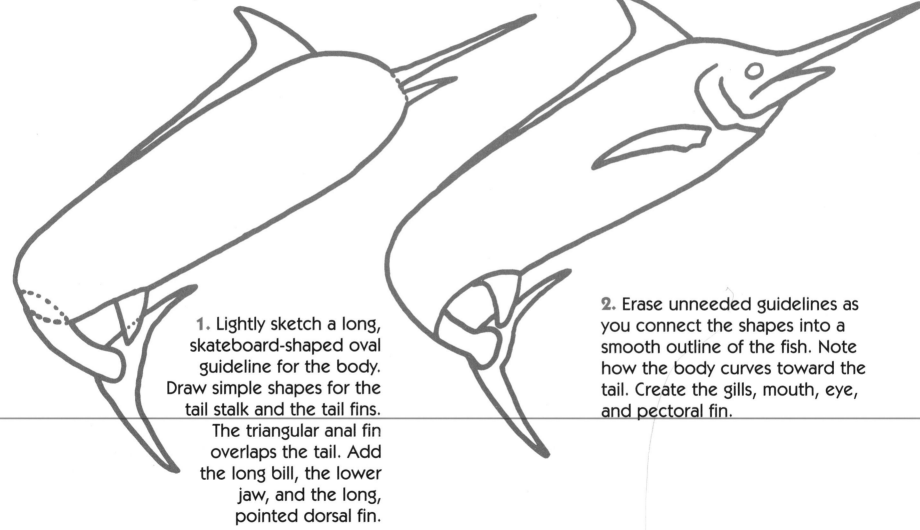

1. Lightly sketch a long, skateboard-shaped oval guideline for the body. Draw simple shapes for the tail stalk and the tail fins. The triangular anal fin overlaps the tail. Add the long bill, the lower jaw, and the long, pointed dorsal fin.

2. Erase unneeded guidelines as you connect the shapes into a smooth outline of the fish. Note how the body curves toward the tail. Create the gills, mouth, eye, and pectoral fin.

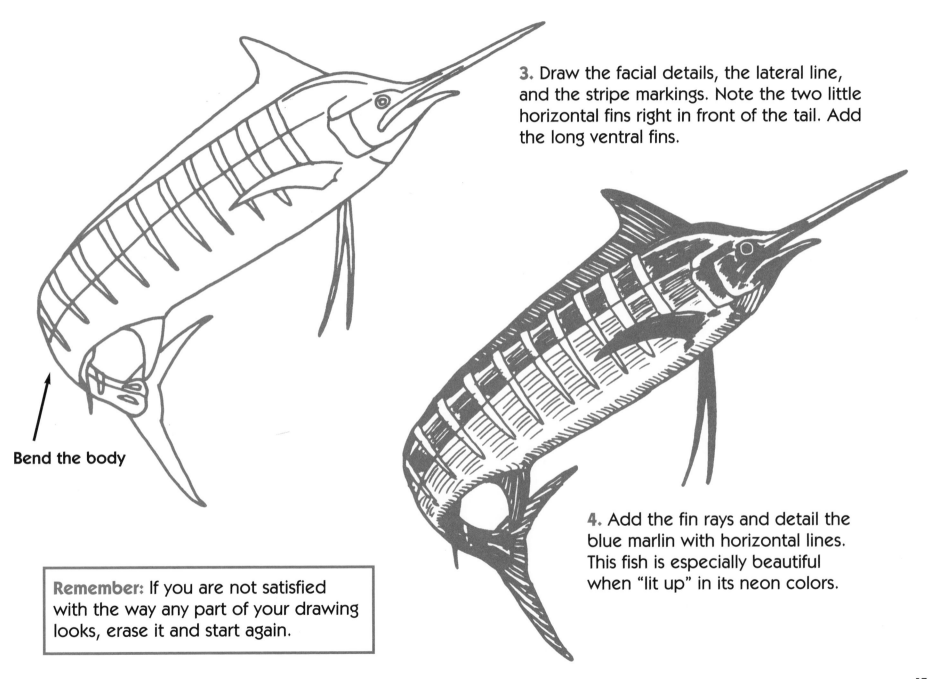

3. Draw the facial details, the lateral line, and the stripe markings. Note the two little horizontal fins right in front of the tail. Add the long ventral fins.

4. Add the fin rays and detail the blue marlin with horizontal lines. This fish is especially beautiful when "lit up" in its neon colors.

Bend the body

Remember: If you are not satisfied with the way any part of your drawing looks, erase it and start again.

Moray Eel

A five-foot green moray eel, with its mouth open and sharp teeth bared, can be a threatening sight. But the eel rarely attacks people. In fact, it can be quite calm, sometimes allowing itself to be fed and stroked by divers. Moray eels are shy. They prefer to live in coral caves and other hiding places.

1. Draw two rounded, overlapping rectangular shapes to form the moray's body. Add shapes for the beak, eye, and triangular tail.

Add dorsal ridge

2. Smooth and form the outline, erasing the overlapping guidelines. Outline the dorsal fin, noting how it wraps around the tail. Draw the tiny gill opening, the mouth, and the eye.

Connect and round

Connect and round

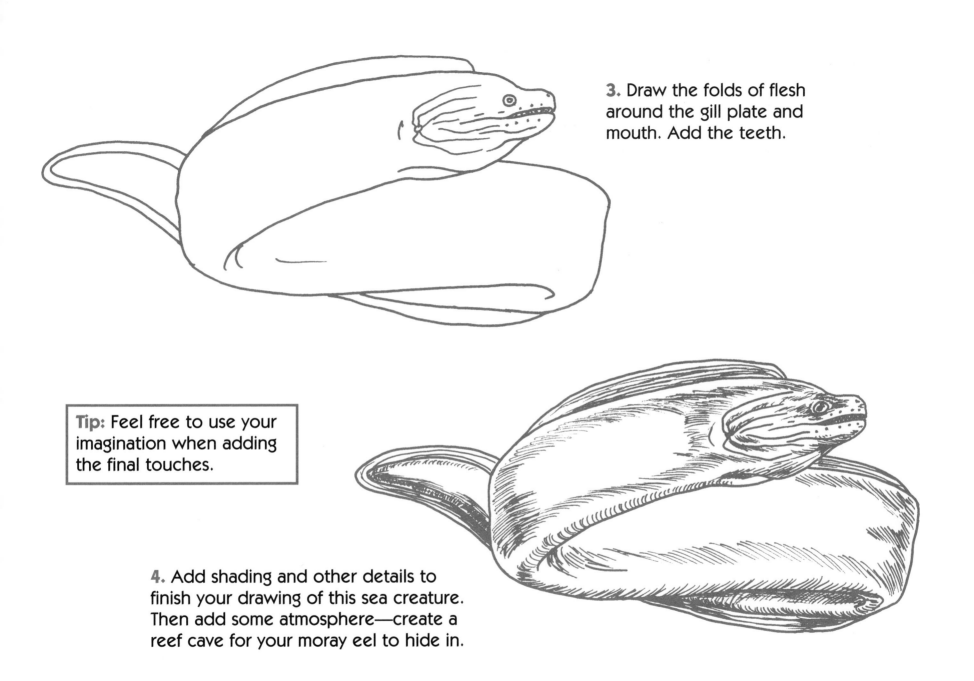

3. Draw the folds of flesh around the gill plate and mouth. Add the teeth.

Tip: Feel free to use your imagination when adding the final touches.

4. Add shading and other details to finish your drawing of this sea creature. Then add some atmosphere—create a reef cave for your moray eel to hide in.

Purple-spotted Sea Goddess

This sea slug, or nudibranch (NOO-de-brank), lives on reefs in the Caribbean Sea. (*Nudibranch* means "naked gills.") The rare, little sea creature grows to two inches in length, and is rusty brown with white edges and little purple spots. It eats the algae that grows on coral.

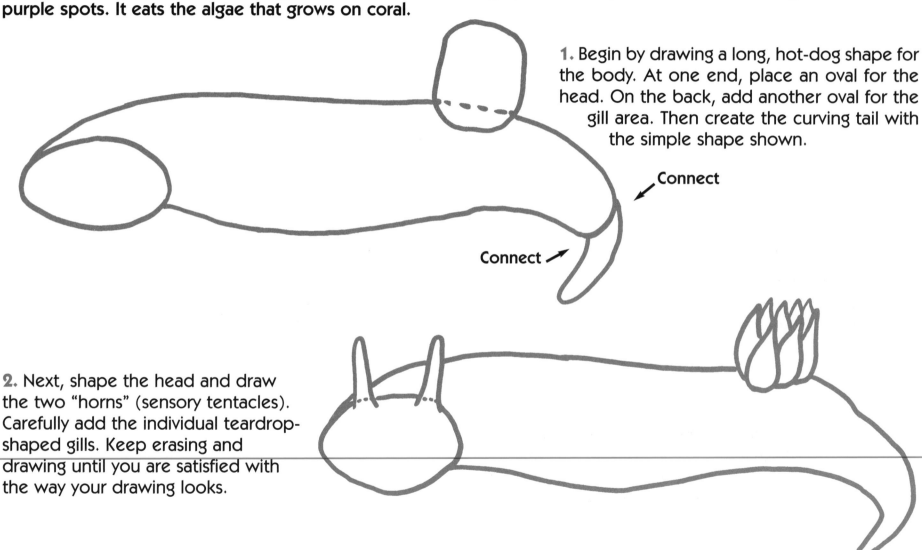

1. Begin by drawing a long, hot-dog shape for the body. At one end, place an oval for the head. On the back, add another oval for the gill area. Then create the curving tail with the simple shape shown.

Connect

Connect

2. Next, shape the head and draw the two "horns" (sensory tentacles). Carefully add the individual teardrop-shaped gills. Keep erasing and drawing until you are satisfied with the way your drawing looks.

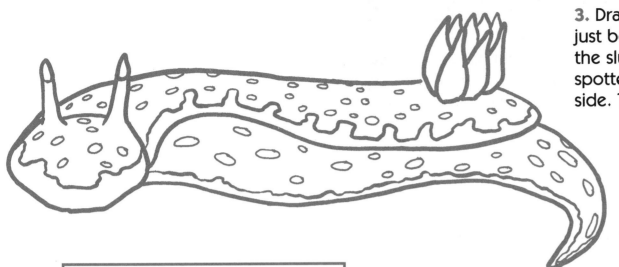

3. Draw a curved line from the head to just beyond the gills. The line separates the slug's back from its side. Outline the spotted areas on the head, back, and side. Then start adding the spots.

Tip: No one gets it right the first time! Erasing and redrawing are important parts of the process.

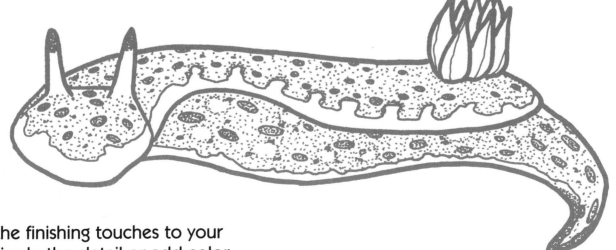

4. To add the finishing touches to your drawing, stipple the detail or add color.

Great Hammerhead Shark

Although the great hammerhead shark is considered dangerous, it rarely approaches people aggressively. This unusual-looking shark is silvery gray on its upper body and light below. The largest of the hammerheads, the great hammerhead can grow to 18 feet.

1. Start with a long, surfboard-shaped oval for the body. On top of the head, attach a thin rectangular shape, and directly behind, a tall triangle for the dorsal fin. Add a boomerang shape for the tail, then add all the other fins, as shown.

2. Combine the shapes into a smooth outline of the shark, shaping the fins and the "hammer." Erase any guidelines you no longer need.

Remember: Until the last step, keep all your pencil lines light and soft, so they will be easier to erase later.

3. Add a lobe to the upper part of the tail, as shown. Draw the mouth and gill slits. At the end of the "hammer," add an eye.

4. Add details and shading to complete your drawing. Crosshatching or stippling work well. For a realistic look, draw a whole bunch of hammerheads—these sharks often swim in large schools.

Hermit Crab

Unlike a true crab, a hermit crab cannot make its own shell. It must find an abandoned shell to protect its soft body. When the hermit outgrows one shell, it moves out and finds a larger one.

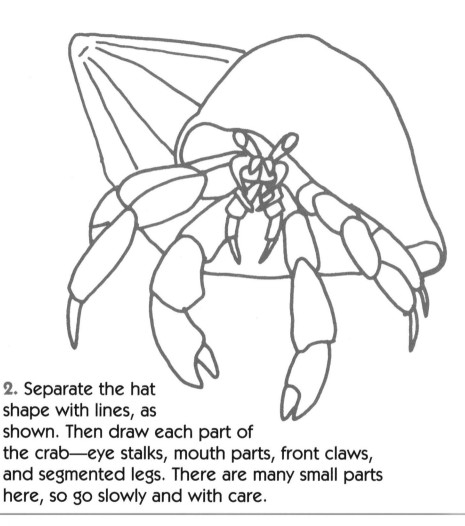

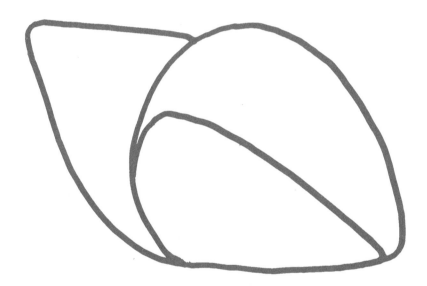

1. Begin with a large oval. Then draw a curved line through it, almost cutting it in half. Add a triangular "hat" on the left side of the oval.

2. Separate the hat shape with lines, as shown. Then draw each part of the crab—eye stalks, mouth parts, front claws, and segmented legs. There are many small parts here, so go slowly and with care.

Tip: Focus on one part at a time, breaking it down into basic shapes and simple lines.

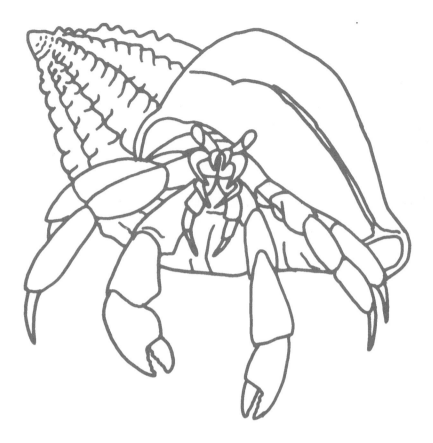

3. Start adding details the top of the shell with whorls and bumps, as shown. Take your time! Note the shapes in the large part of the shell and underneath the crab's claws.

4. Detail the hermit crab with lines, stippling, or crosshatching. If you follow the curve of the shell as you add details, you will have a more realistic drawing.

Octopus

The shy reef octopus is a member of a large family of octopuses that range in size from a couple of inches to several feet. Octopuses change color and even grow warts to suit their emotional state. The changing colors helps camouflage them from predators. Although the 20-inch reef octopus's color varies, it usually has a blue-green body with rust-colored mottling.

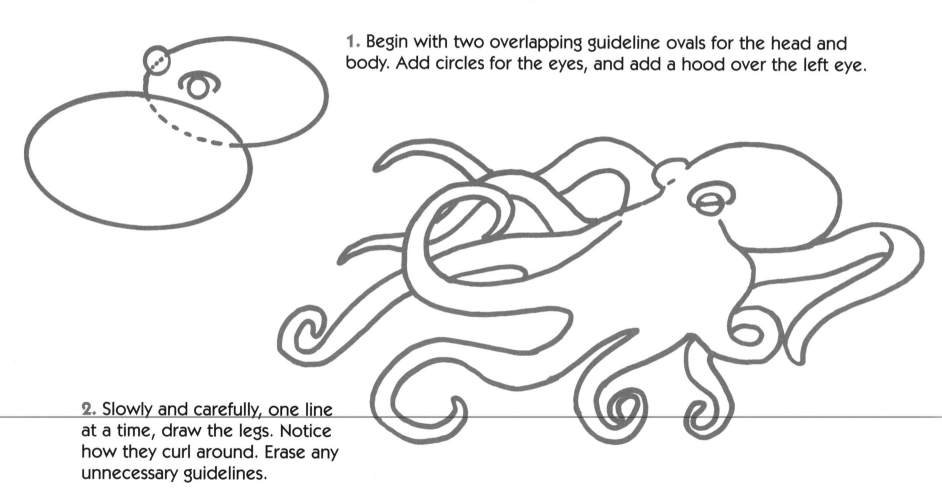

1. Begin with two overlapping guideline ovals for the head and body. Add circles for the eyes, and add a hood over the left eye.

2. Slowly and carefully, one line at a time, draw the legs. Notice how they curl around. Erase any unnecessary guidelines.

3. Draw the flat bottom on each tentacle, taking note of the curling ends. Draw the markings, paying attention to the curve of the arms and head.

Tip: If something looks complex, focus on one part at a time. Breaking it down into basic shapes and simple lines will make it easier to draw.

4. Create the suction cups on the tentacles by drawing two tiny circles next to each other. Finish your octopus by completing the markings with stippling. This drawing will really give you a sense of accomplishment!

Rainbow Parrotfish

Parrotfish are named for their bright colors and the strong beaks that they use to scrape and feed on coral. The colors vary greatly, but in general the head and front section are orange and the back and rear section are green. The tail and other fins may be orange, trimmed with purple.

1. Begin with a large, free-form oval for the body and a smaller one for the head. Two triangles form the ventral fins. Draw an oval guideline for the tail and attach it to the body with simple lines.

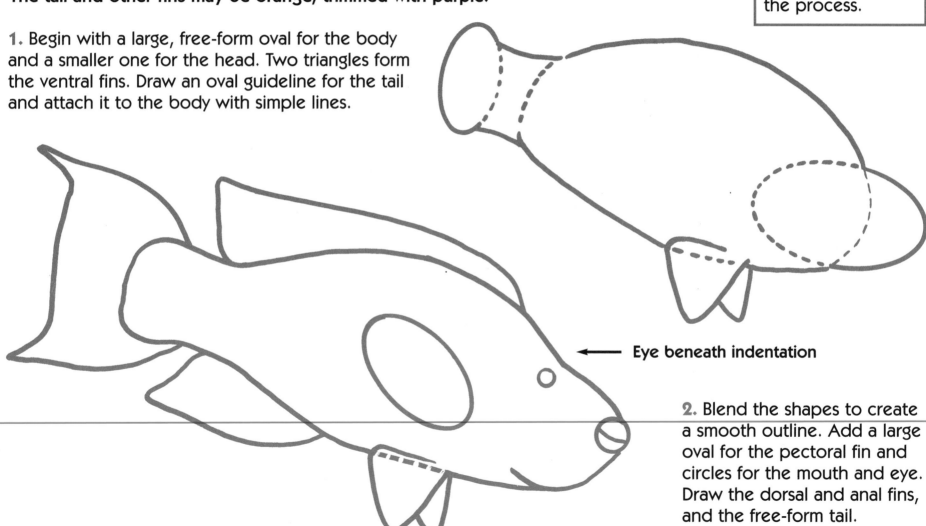

← Eye beneath indentation

2. Blend the shapes to create a smooth outline. Add a large oval for the pectoral fin and circles for the mouth and eye. Draw the dorsal and anal fins, and the free-form tail.

3. Draw the details around the mouth and eye, as shown. Add the gills and shape the fins. Then draw outlines for the body markings.

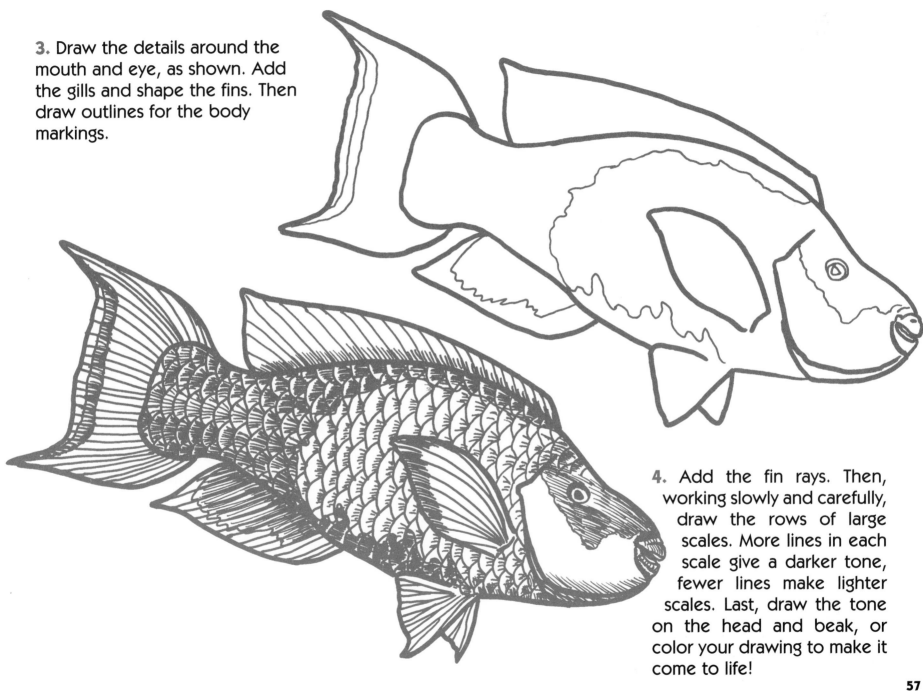

4. Add the fin rays. Then, working slowly and carefully, draw the rows of large scales. More lines in each scale give a darker tone, fewer lines make lighter scales. Last, draw the tone on the head and beak, or color your drawing to make it come to life!

Porcupine Fish

The porcupine fish is a member of the spiny pufferfish family. A pufferfish will inflate with air or water to make itself too large for a predator to swallow. The porcupine fish is yellow and brown on top, with dark polka dots on its white belly. The fish in this drawing is inflated. When not inflated, the fish is smaller and the spines do not stick out.

2. Define the mouth, eye, gill, and fins. Then blend the shapes, erasing the overlapping lines. Take your time with this step, making sure that you are satisfied with it before going on to the next steps.

1. Draw a large, free-form oval for the body. Attach the tail stalk and tail fin. Add a large oval guideline in the center for the pec fin, and the other shapes for the eye, gill, and dorsal fin.

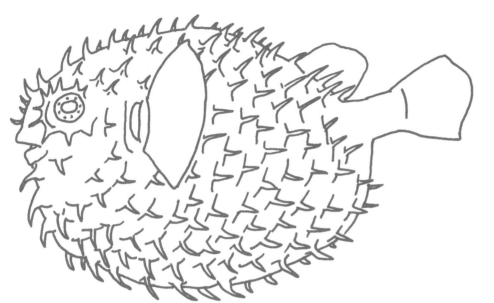

3. Now comes the tricky part. Notice how the spines are in rows, like scales on other fish. Carefully draw the spines and the rest of the details. Notice the ring of spines around the eye and the spiny beard under the chin. Add detail to the eye.

> **Tip:** The spines of porcupine fish are actually modified scales, so draw them in rows, not randomly.

4. Draw the fin rays and darken the gill opening. Add black spots to the back and sides, but not on the belly. Add a little shading along the edge of the belly to complete your drawing. What predator do you think might have caused this porcupine fish to inflate? Draw it next to your porcupine fish.

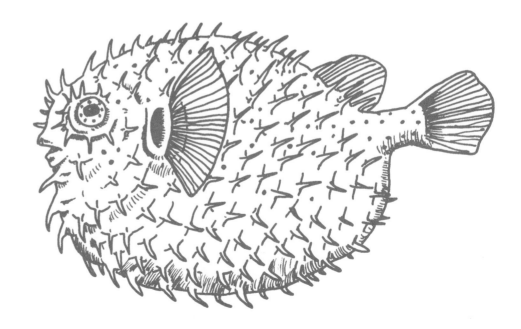

Sea Horse

The sea horse lives in all temperate and tropical oceans. It comes in a variety of colors and patterns. Many sea horses are colored to match the corals and plants they hang on to as they feed on plankton.

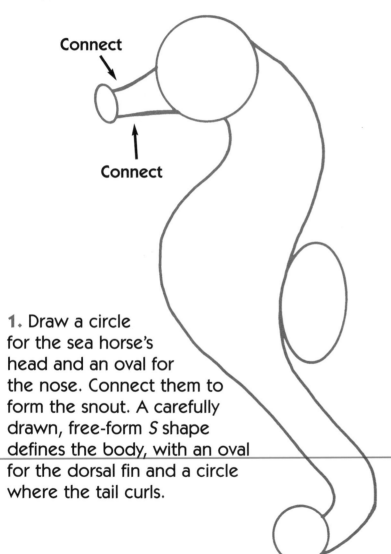

Connect

Connect

1. Draw a circle for the sea horse's head and an oval for the nose. Connect them to form the snout. A carefully drawn, free-form *S* shape defines the body, with an oval for the dorsal fin and a circle where the tail curls.

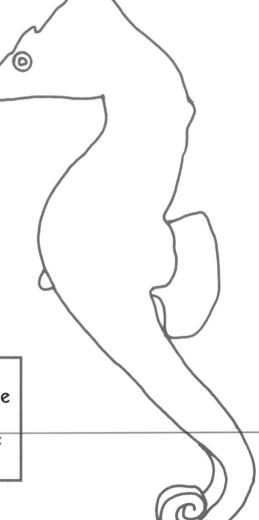

2. Combine, blend, and define the shapes. Form the head, add the eye, curl the tip of the tail, and shape the dorsal fin. Erase any guidelines you no longer need.

Tip: Don't be intimidated by the complicated design of the sea horse. Just be patient, and remember to take it one basic shape at a time.

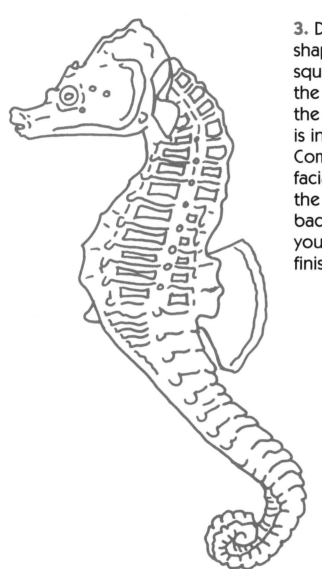

3. Draw the rectangular shapes, tiny circles, and squiggly lines all over the body. Notice that the outline of the body is indented or rippled. Complete the head and facial features, adding the pectoral fin at the back of the head. Now you are ready for the finishing touches.

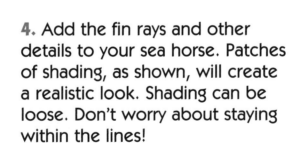

4. Add the fin rays and other details to your sea horse. Patches of shading, as shown, will create a realistic look. Shading can be loose. Don't worry about staying within the lines!

Sperm Whale

The sperm whale, the largest of the toothed whales, can grow to 60 feet in length. Found in all oceans, this deep-diving champion can dive as deep as 3,000 feet in search of prey! Sperm whales are dark gray with some white markings on the lower jaw and sometimes on the belly.

1. Lightly draw a large, rounded rectangle for the central part of the body. Add the overlapping rectangular head, and a fingerlike shape for the lower jaw. Then, for the back section of the body attach a cone shape that tapers to the tail. Add the fins, and a triangle for the flukes.

2. Blend the shapes into a smooth outline of the whale's body. Erase overlapping guidelines. Note the eye above the corner of the mouth.

3. Sketch the outline markings for the white color on the jaws and belly. Then draw the lines down the side, where the skin is wrinkled. Add the bottom teeth.

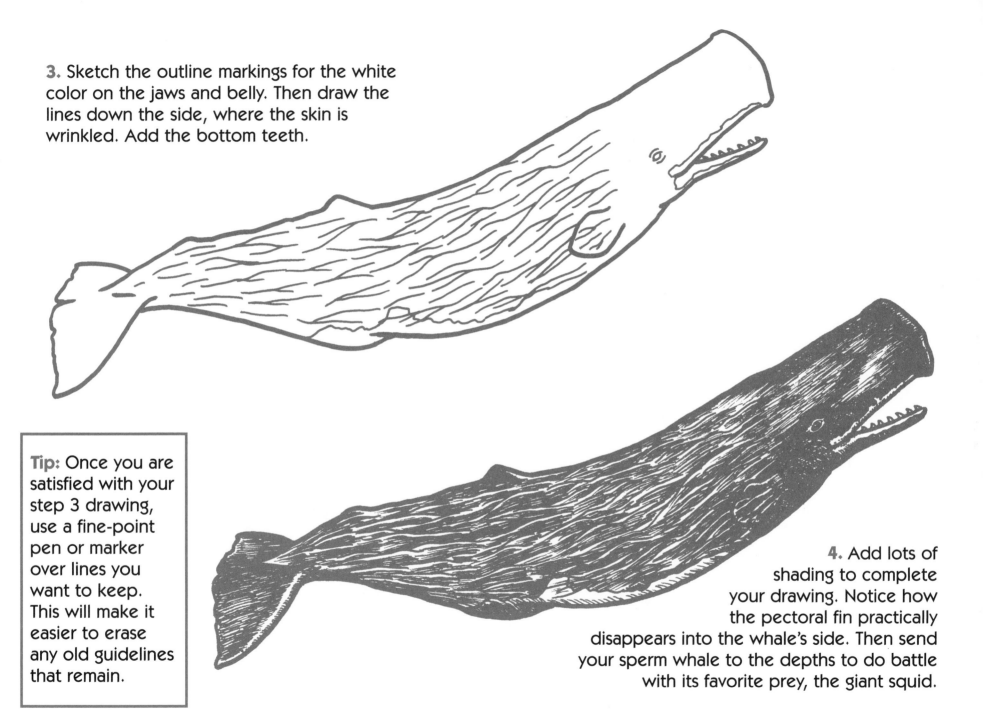

Tip: Once you are satisfied with your step 3 drawing, use a fine-point pen or marker over lines you want to keep. This will make it easier to erase any old guidelines that remain.

4. Add lots of shading to complete your drawing. Notice how the pectoral fin practically disappears into the whale's side. Then send your sperm whale to the depths to do battle with its favorite prey, the giant squid.

Giant Squid

Like other squid, this sea creature has well-developed eyes, eight arms, two longer sucker arms, and the ability to change color when threatened. Unlike other squid, the giant squid can grow to 60 feet in length! No one has ever seen a live specimen, because the giant squid lives in the dark ocean depths. But beached ones appear to be reddish orange in color.

Tip: Studying the step 4 drawing before you start will help you understand what you will be doing in steps 1, 2, and 3.

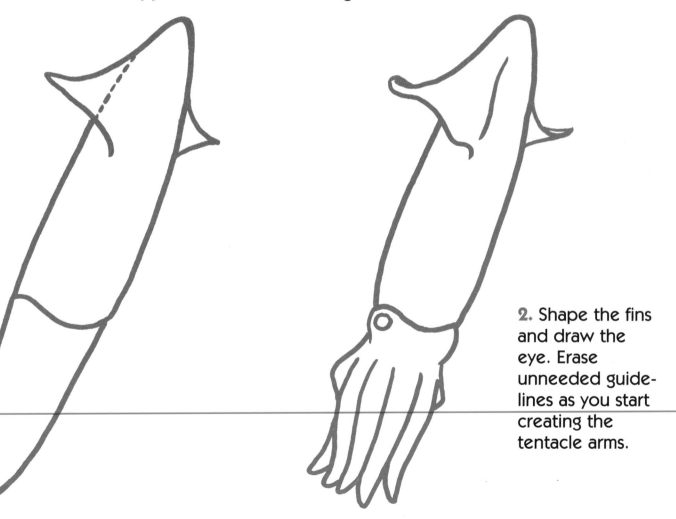

1. Draw a long surfboard guide-line shape and divide it in two. Add the triangular fins at one end.

2. Shape the fins and draw the eye. Erase unneeded guide-lines as you start creating the tentacle arms.

3. Draw the two long sucker arms, then start adding the spot markings. Once you are satisfied with your drawing, you are ready to add the finishing touches.

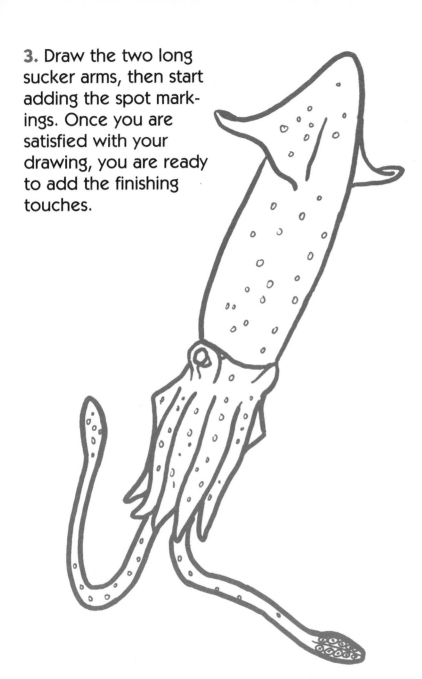

4. Stipple the shading and add the details on the giant squid. Then send it to the depths to do battle with your sperm whale.

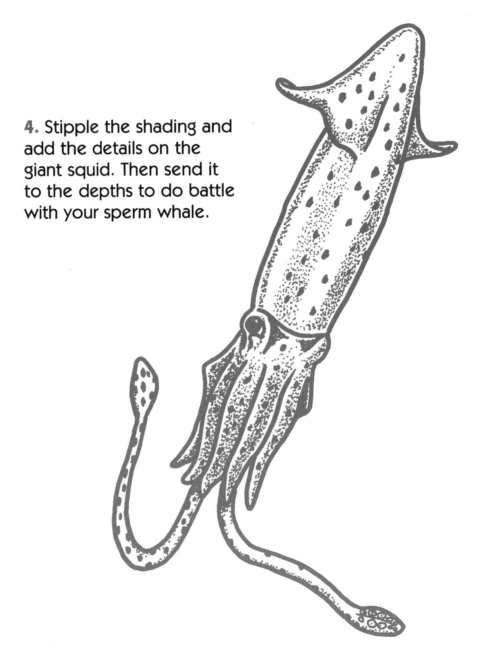

Yellowfin Tuna

Yellowfin tuna live in huge schools in all temperate and tropical oceans. This speedy game fish can grow to 6 feet and weigh up to 300 pounds. It has a dark blue back, silvery sides, and yellow fins.

1. Begin with a large, free-form oval for the main part of the body. At the front, add a cone shape for the head. Behind, add a triangle for the tail stalk.

Remember: Always draw your guidelines lightly in steps 1. and 2. They will be easier to erase later.

2. Erase the overlapping lines. Then blend and smooth the body shapes. Add a crescent shape for the tail and the other simple shapes for the fins. Draw the eye, mouth, and gill plate.

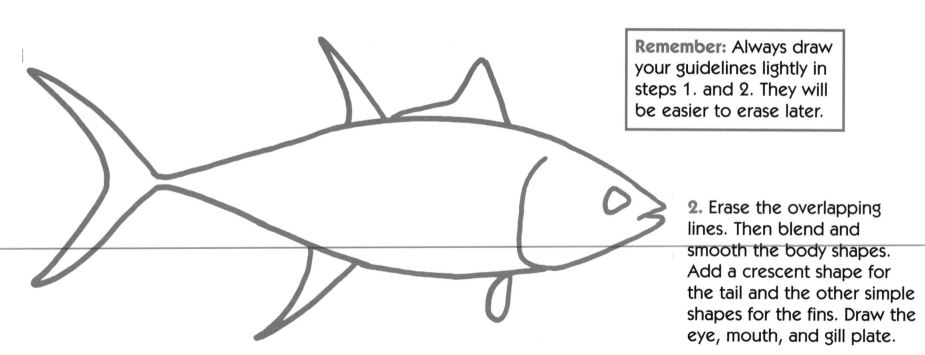

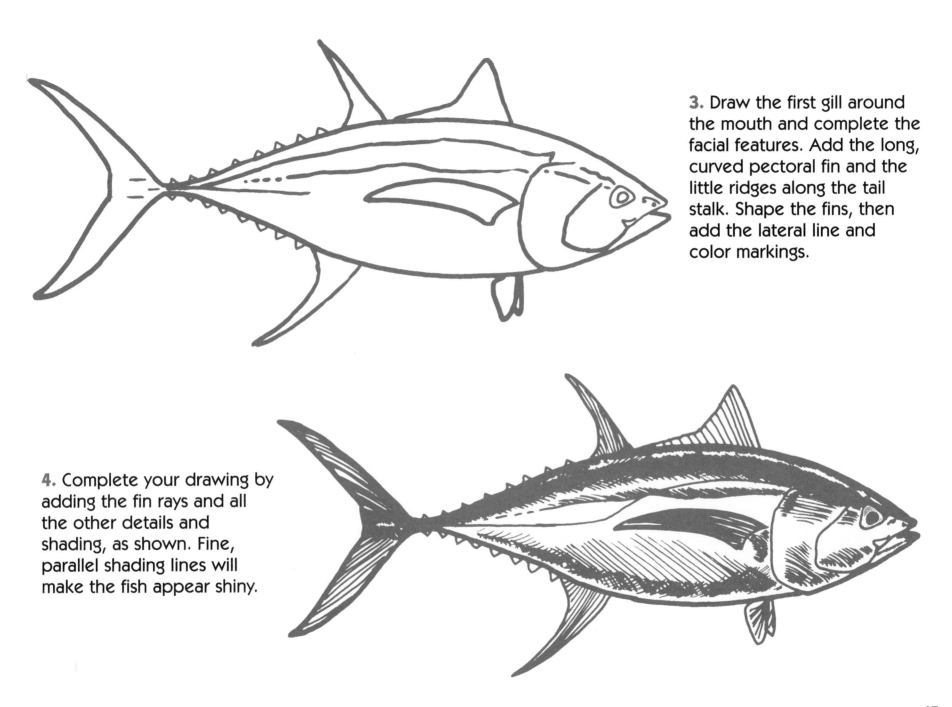

3. Draw the first gill around the mouth and complete the facial features. Add the long, curved pectoral fin and the little ridges along the tail stalk. Shape the fins, then add the lateral line and color markings.

4. Complete your drawing by adding the fin rays and all the other details and shading, as shown. Fine, parallel shading lines will make the fish appear shiny.

Viperfish

The 12-inch-long silver-colored viperfish has its own lights to attract prey in the deepest depths of the ocean. Beneath the lighted lure on the first spine of its dorsal fin, the viperfish has large, transparent teeth that prey don't see until it's too late. It also has a bony projection, with a light on the end of it, inside its mouth.

1. Start by lightly drawing a large, long, curving oval for the body. At one end, draw smaller ovals to start the head and the bony projection in the fish's mouth. At the other end, add a rounded cone that overlaps the body shape, as shown.

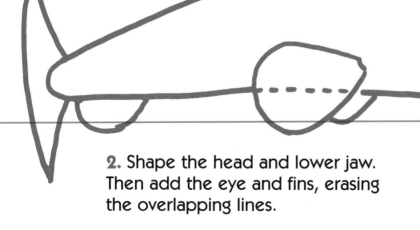

2. Shape the head and lower jaw. Then add the eye and fins, erasing the overlapping lines.

Remember: It is easy to draw almost anything if you first build a good foundation.

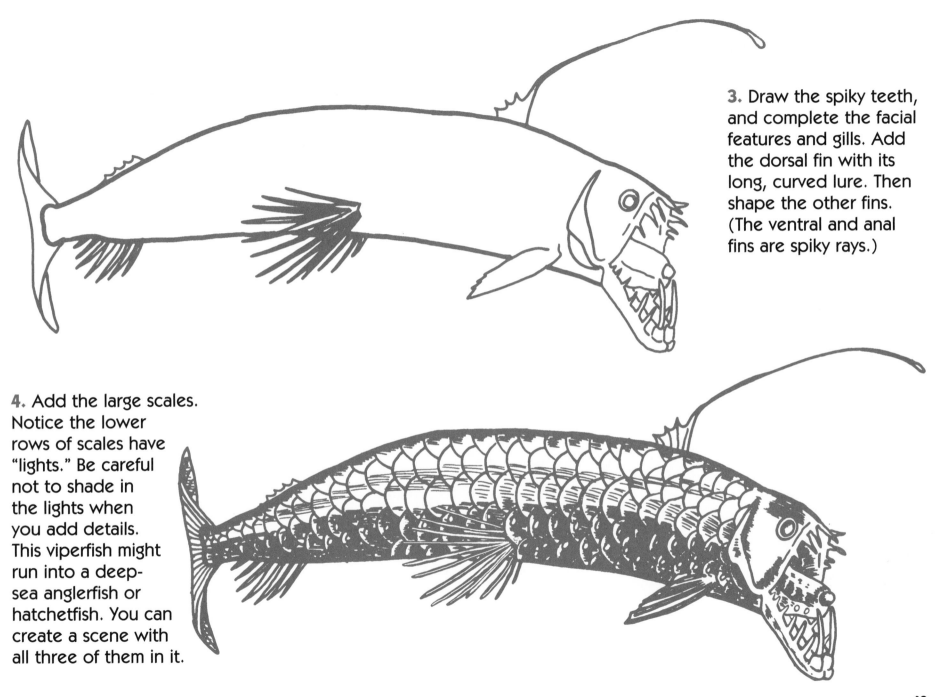

3. Draw the spiky teeth, and complete the facial features and gills. Add the dorsal fin with its long, curved lure. Then shape the other fins. (The ventral and anal fins are spiky rays.)

4. Add the large scales. Notice the lower rows of scales have "lights." Be careful not to shade in the lights when you add details. This viperfish might run into a deep-sea anglerfish or hatchetfish. You can create a scene with all three of them in it.

Whale Shark

The whale shark is the largest fish in the world. It can grow to be more than 40 feet long. A gentle, plankton filter-feeder, the whale shark often lets swimmers and divers touch it and hang on to its giant dorsal fin for a ride. Long ridges run along its back, and its brownish, blue-gray coloration is dotted with rows of large, white square spots.

1. Start with a large, free-form oval for the front part of the huge body. Add the triangular shapes for the tail stalk, tail, and fins.

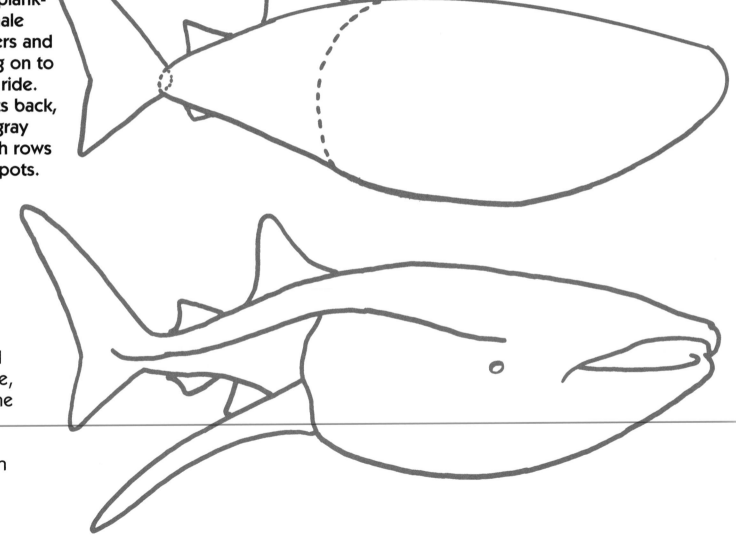

2. Blend the shapes and smooth the body outline, rounding and forming the fins. Draw the eye and mouth. Add the lateral line, and the pectoral fin behind the gill line.

70

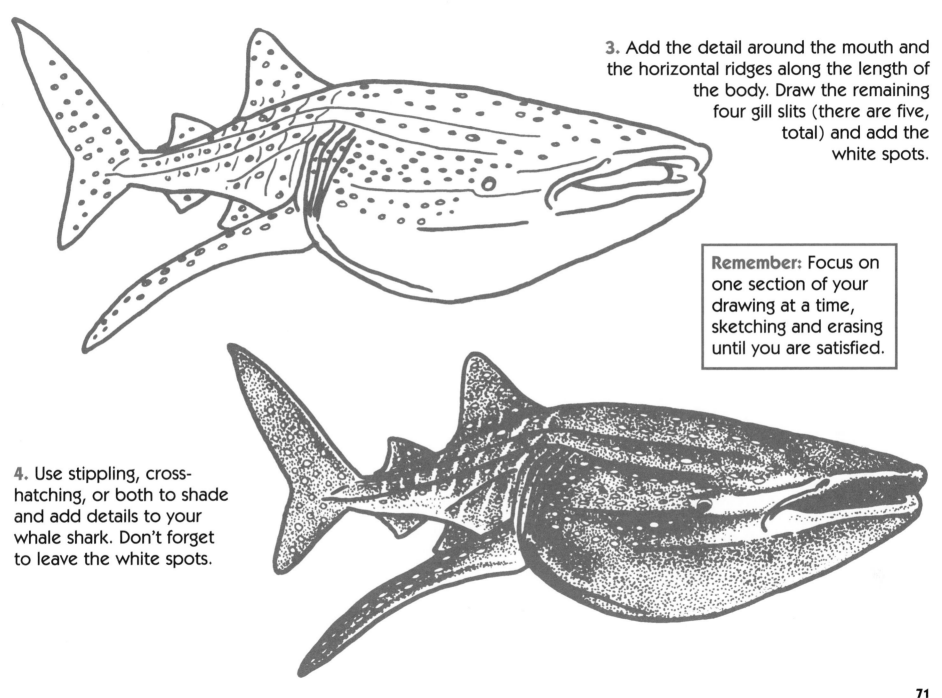

3. Add the detail around the mouth and the horizontal ridges along the length of the body. Draw the remaining four gill slits (there are five, total) and add the white spots.

Remember: Focus on one section of your drawing at a time, sketching and erasing until you are satisfied.

4. Use stippling, cross-hatching, or both to shade and add details to your whale shark. Don't forget to leave the white spots.

Portuguese Man-o'-war

The Portuguese man-o'-war has no way to move itself, so it floats at the surface of the warm Atlantic Ocean. This jellyfish's large, gas-filled bubble is moved by the winds and tides. Hidden beneath the bubble are many long, poisonous tentacles, which may be 30 feet in length. The Portuguese man-o'-war's bubble is pinkish purple. The tentacles are pink and dark red.

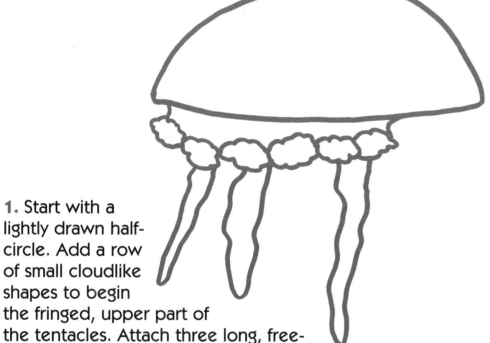

1. Start with a lightly drawn half-circle. Add a row of small cloudlike shapes to begin the fringed, upper part of the tentacles. Attach three long, free-form shapes for the main tentacles.

2. Shape the bubble. Start adding the curving fringe to the tentacles, and erase and redraw to blend the cloud shapes into a smooth, clean body outline.

Tip: This fish's tentacles are irregular and may be drawn at random. The ones shown here just give you a general idea of how they look. Feel free to draw yours as you wish.

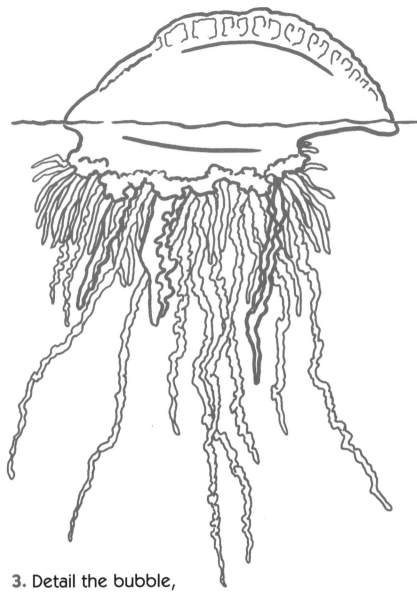

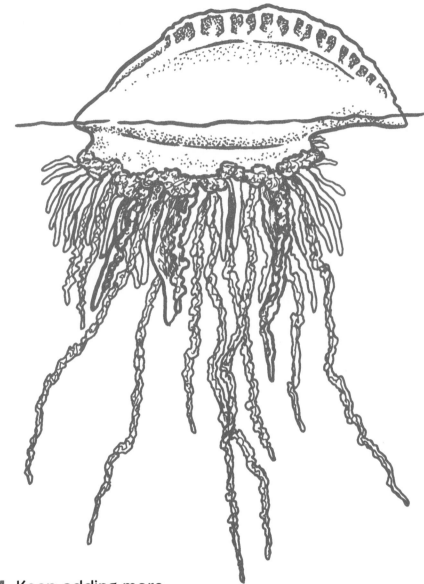

3. Detail the bubble,
which is pinched at the
top to form more of a sail. Draw many tentacles
(more than you see here, if you wish). Some are
short, smooth projections, while others are very long.

4. Keep adding more
details. Little scribbles on the long tentacles are all
you need, plus a little stippling, to help shape the
bubble and give it some dimension.

Pacific Sockeye Salmon

When a male sockeye salmon leaves the ocean and enters freshwater rivers, his body begins to change. He gets a hump in his back and his jaws get longer. Both male and female sockeyes swim upstream to breed—in the same stream where they were hatched—then they die. The sockeye grows to three feet. It has a bright red body, pale green head, and lighter belly.

1. Begin with free-form oval guidelines for the body, head, and tail stalk. Notice the line for the gills. Add the clawlike mouth, pectoral and tail fins, and a circle for the eye.

2. Shape the head, then blend the body shapes into a smooth outline of the salmon. Erase unneeded guidelines. Add the dorsal, ventral, and anal fins.

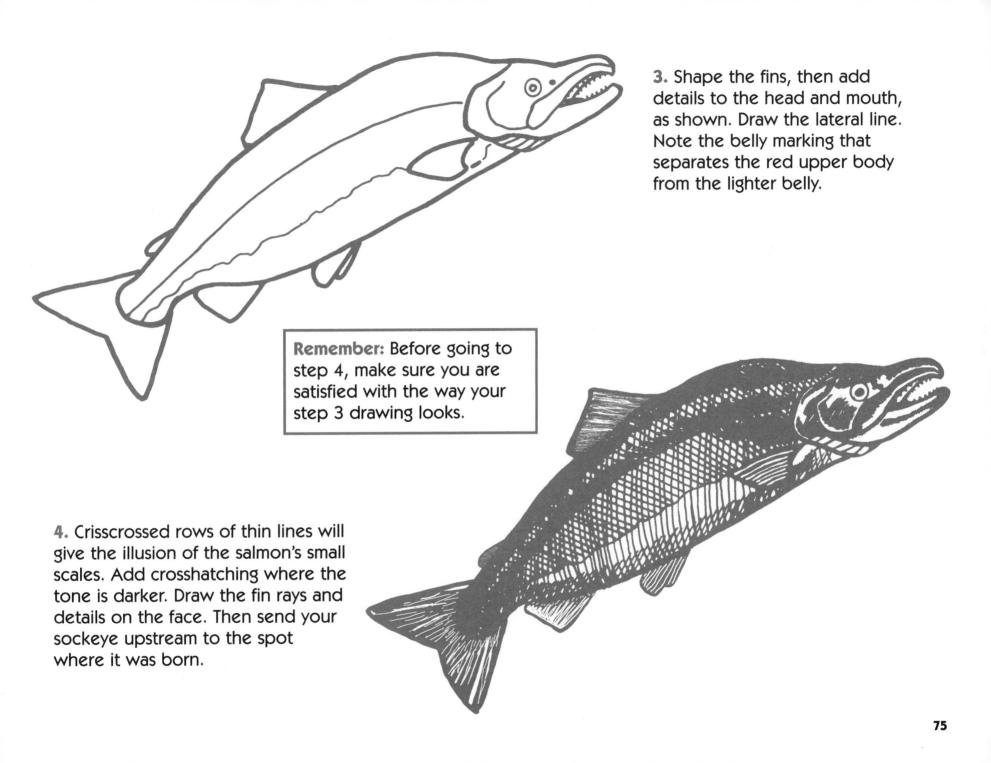

3. Shape the fins, then add details to the head and mouth, as shown. Draw the lateral line. Note the belly marking that separates the red upper body from the lighter belly.

Remember: Before going to step 4, make sure you are satisfied with the way your step 3 drawing looks.

4. Crisscrossed rows of thin lines will give the illusion of the salmon's small scales. Add crosshatching where the tone is darker. Draw the fin rays and details on the face. Then send your sockeye upstream to the spot where it was born.

Southern Stingray

The southern stingray is brown to gray on its back and white underneath. On five-foot-long wings, it glides just above the bottom of the ocean, from New England to North Florida, feeding on mollusks and crustaceans (shellfish). A large poisonous stinger is located at the base of this fish's tail. When injected into a predator or human, the poison causes severe pain.

1. Draw a large, free-form oval for the stingray's body. Attach a long, thin rectangle for the tail. Note the triangular stinger.

2. Shape the pointed wings and blend the tail stalk with the body. Add a line down the middle, and on either side draw the eye sockets.

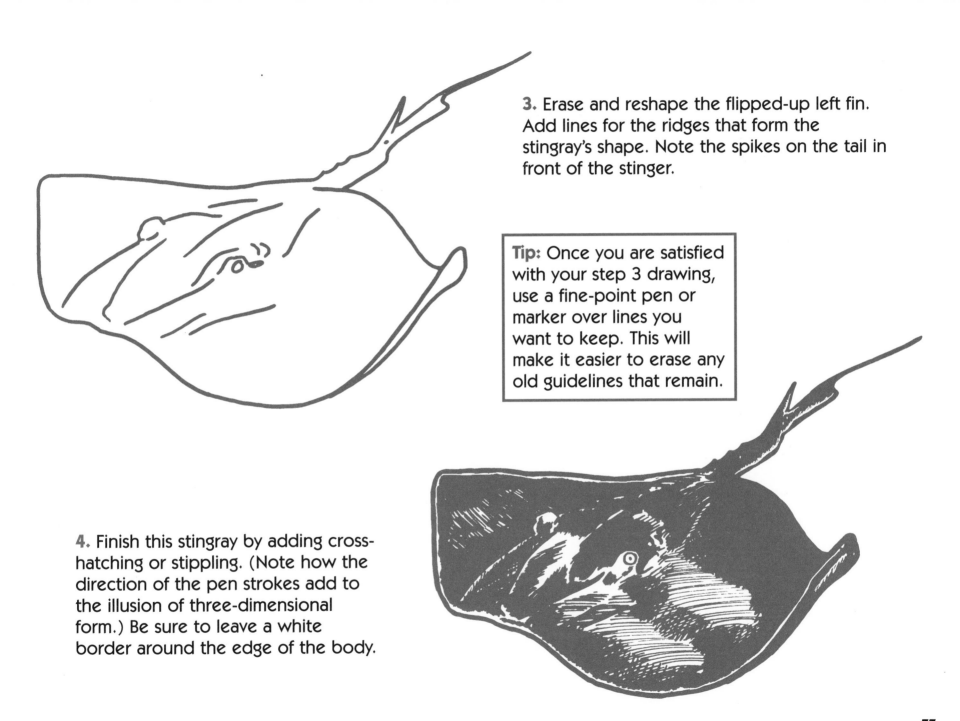

3. Erase and reshape the flipped-up left fin. Add lines for the ridges that form the stingray's shape. Note the spikes on the tail in front of the stinger.

Tip: Once you are satisfied with your step 3 drawing, use a fine-point pen or marker over lines you want to keep. This will make it easier to erase any old guidelines that remain.

4. Finish this stingray by adding cross-hatching or stippling. (Note how the direction of the pen strokes add to the illusion of three-dimensional form.) Be sure to leave a white border around the edge of the body.

Beta

Also known as the Siamese fighting fish, the little two-and-a-half-inch-long beta is a brightly colored freshwater fish from southeastern Asia. When challenged, the male (shown here) sticks out its gill plates to make himself look larger and fiercer, and attacks his challenger. A beta kept as a pet may display the same fierce behavior toward a human's finger in its tank.

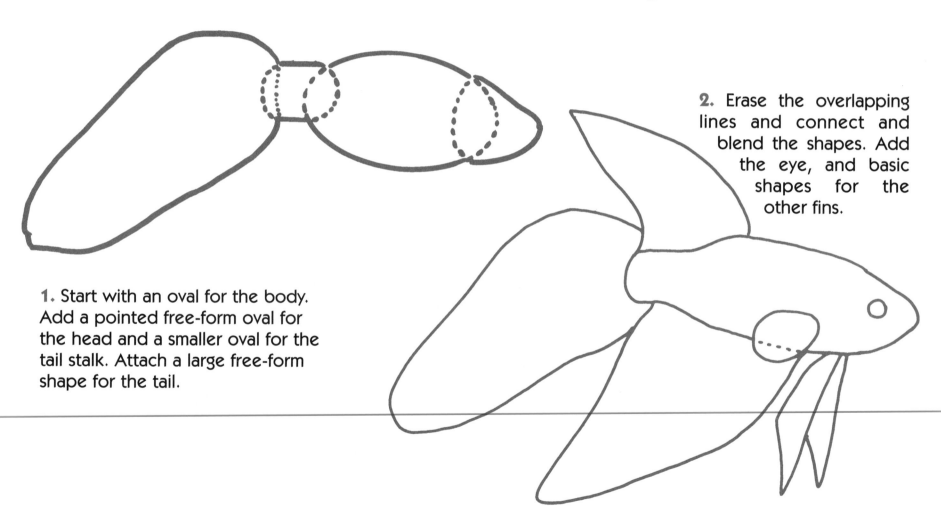

2. Erase the overlapping lines and connect and blend the shapes. Add the eye, and basic shapes for the other fins.

1. Start with an oval for the body. Add a pointed free-form oval for the head and a smaller oval for the tail stalk. Attach a large free-form shape for the tail.

3. Draw the mouth and gills, and add detail to the eye. Rough out the fins, making the edges ragged.

> **Tip:** Start in the middle of the fin when you begin to draw the rays. Make the fin rays wave to match the ripples in the beta's fins.

4. Add the rows of scales and the fin rays. Add the detail with thin, parallel lines. (It may look difficult, but it isn't.) Draw the rounded form of the fish by adding more shading on the belly scales and less in the middle. If you want to add color, a male beta is bright red, blue, or a mixture of different colors.

Manta Ray

A relative of the shark, the giant manta ray glides through the water on wings that can reach 20 feet across. Harmless to humans, the manta ray feeds on plankton. It directs the flow of tiny organisms into its mouth with two flexible fins that project from either side.

2. Smooth the outline while erasing unneeded guidelines. Draw the eye and whiplike tail, and outline the spot markings. Draw the gills. (The five gills on each side indicate that the manta ray is a member of the shark family.)

Remember: Breaking things down into basic shapes and lines makes them easier to draw.

1. Draw a free-form oval for the body, two triangular wing shapes, and the long fins around the mouth. Add the oval anal fins.

3. Darken the eye, then complete your manta ray with light shading. The bottom (shown) is mostly white with light gray spots.

Mola-mola

Also known as the ocean sunfish for its surface-basking behavior, this giant sea creature can grow to 13 feet in length and weigh as much as 3,300 pounds. It inhabits the surface of most open seas. Mola-molas are brown to gray-blue on the back, and metallic silver on the sides and belly.

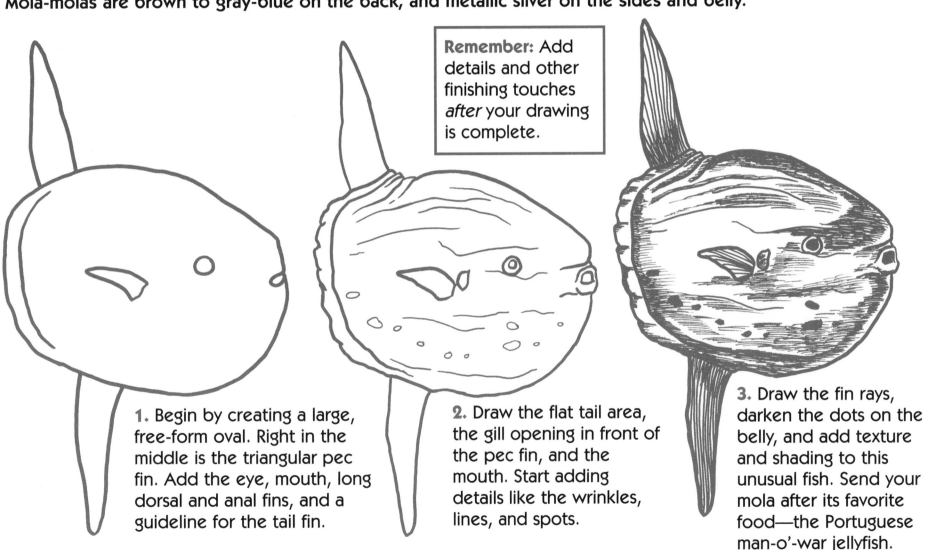

Remember: Add details and other finishing touches *after* your drawing is complete.

1. Begin by creating a large, free-form oval. Right in the middle is the triangular pec fin. Add the eye, mouth, long dorsal and anal fins, and a guideline for the tail fin.

2. Draw the flat tail area, the gill opening in front of the pec fin, and the mouth. Start adding details like the wrinkles, lines, and spots.

3. Draw the fin rays, darken the dots on the belly, and add texture and shading to this unusual fish. Send your mola after its favorite food—the Portuguese man-o'-war jellyfish.

Sargassum Triggerfish

The Sargassum triggerfish lives in reefs and offshore banks in the Atlantic, from North Carolina to Brazil. The first dorsal fin of the triggerfish is a sharp spine that protects it from predators. The triggerfish is blue to brownish gray, with black horizontal rows of spots, and a white crescent above the eyes.

1. Create the body with a lightly drawn, tear-shaped oval. Add the rectangular fins and triangular tail. A small oval in the center indicates the pectoral fin, and a circle above the fin marks the eye.

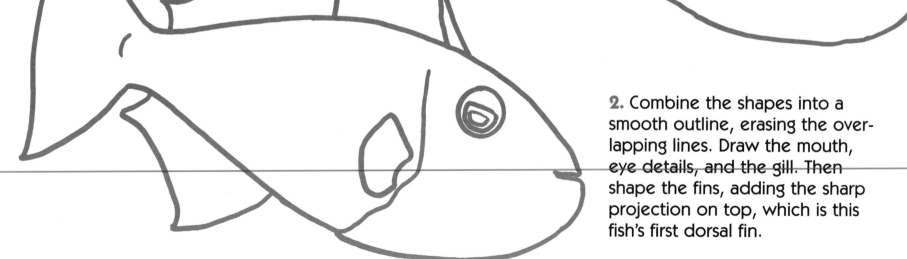

2. Combine the shapes into a smooth outline, erasing the overlapping lines. Draw the mouth, eye details, and the gill. Then shape the fins, adding the sharp projection on top, which is this fish's first dorsal fin.

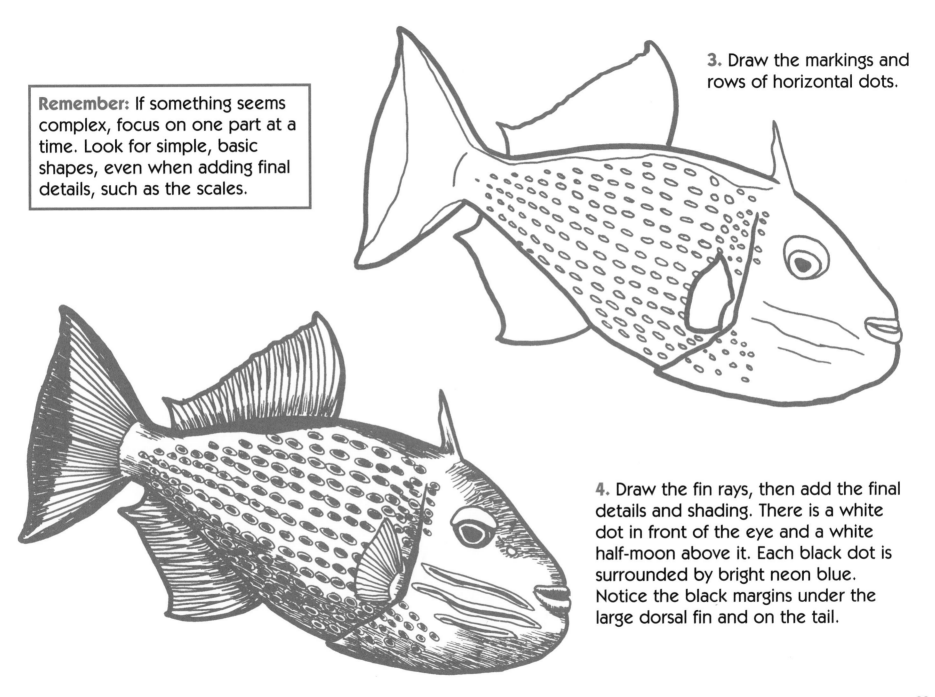

Remember: If something seems complex, focus on one part at a time. Look for simple, basic shapes, even when adding final details, such as the scales.

3. Draw the markings and rows of horizontal dots.

4. Draw the fin rays, then add the final details and shading. There is a white dot in front of the eye and a white half-moon above it. Each black dot is surrounded by bright neon blue. Notice the black margins under the large dorsal fin and on the tail.

Walrus

The walrus is a member of the pinniped (PIN-a-ped) family, which includes seals and sea lions. (*Pinniped* means "feather-footed.") This Arctic resident grows to 12 feet in length and can weigh 3,500 pounds. The walrus uses the two large ivory tusks that grow from its top jaw for hauling itself out of the water and onto ice floes and rocks. Both male and female walruses have tusks.

1. For this drawing, it will be easier to start with the smaller shapes. Beginning with the head, sketch a circle inside a circle and add two small ovals for the "mustache." Add a large circle for the front of the body, and a rounded cone for the back. Then attach the guideline shapes for the flippers.

2. Blend and combine the guideline shapes into a smooth outline of the body. Erase any necessary lines. Start drawing the facial features and long tusks. Notice that the eyes are far apart.

Remember: Take your time doing steps 1 and 2. If you get the basic foundation right, the rest of your drawing will be easy to do.

3. Complete the facial details. Draw the toes on the flippers, and the wrinkles all over the body. The dots over the mouth represent whiskers.

4. Detail your walrus with light shading. Then put it on a rock or an ice floe to bask in the Arctic sun.

Horn Shark

The four-foot-long horn shark has a white belly and a golden-brown back dotted with dark spots. A sharp spine, or horn, sticks up at the base of each dorsal fin. This shark lives in the Pacific, from central California to the Sea of Cortez. It feeds on crustaceans, which it grinds up with its large, flat teeth. Horn sharks are relatively harmless and frequently kept in aquariums.

1. Begin by drawing two over-lapping oval guidelines for the body, then connect them. At the bottom of the second oval, draw a smaller oval for the pectoral fin. Attach a long, thin rectangle behind the second oval for the tail stalk.

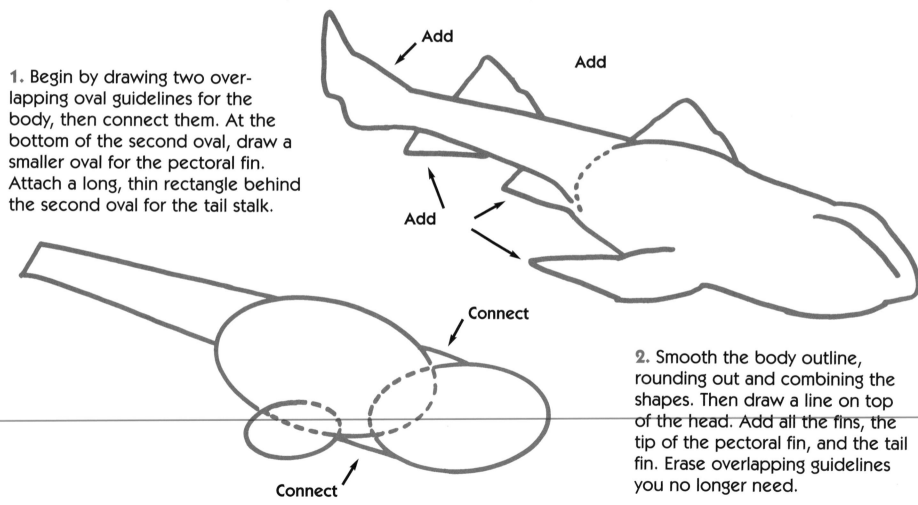

Add

Add

Add

Connect

Connect

2. Smooth the body outline, rounding out and combining the shapes. Then draw a line on top of the head. Add all the fins, the tip of the pectoral fin, and the tail fin. Erase overlapping guidelines you no longer need.

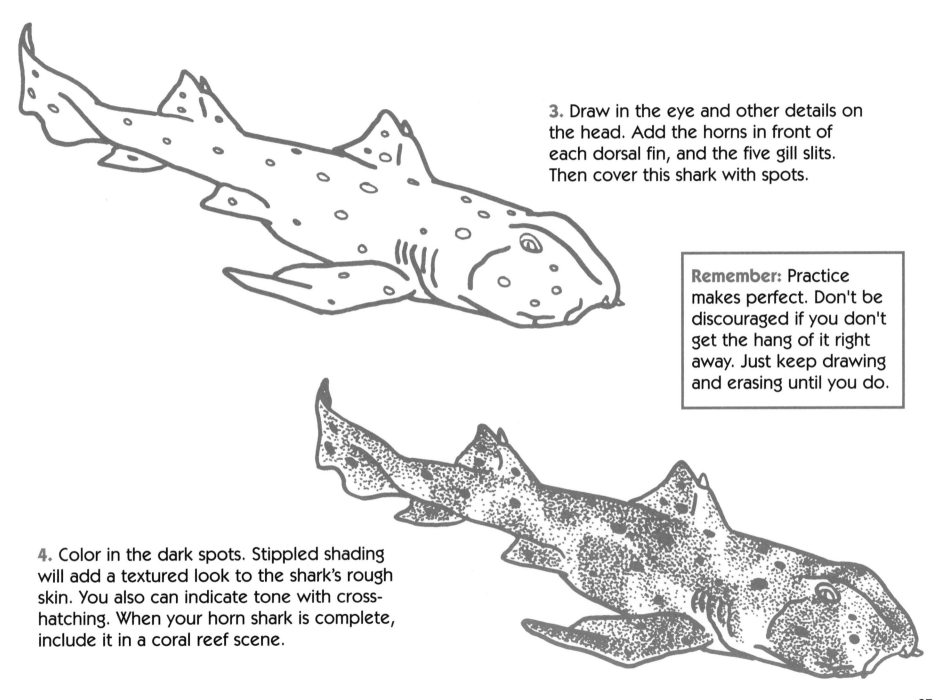

3. Draw in the eye and other details on the head. Add the horns in front of each dorsal fin, and the five gill slits. Then cover this shark with spots.

Remember: Practice makes perfect. Don't be discouraged if you don't get the hang of it right away. Just keep drawing and erasing until you do.

4. Color in the dark spots. Stippled shading will add a textured look to the shark's rough skin. You also can indicate tone with cross-hatching. When your horn shark is complete, include it in a coral reef scene.

Nautilus

The nautilus belongs to an ancient family of marine animals that dates back millions of years. This animal's beautiful, creamy shell with rust colored stripes is highly sought-after by collectors.

Remember: Studying the step 4 drawing before you start will help you understand how the basic shapes relate to each other.

1. Draw a semicircular, free-form guideline shape. Attach a triangular shape at the top end. This is the fleshy lobe. Add an oval in the middle as a guideline for the eye.

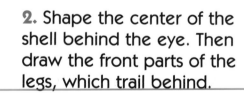

2. Shape the center of the shell behind the eye. Then draw the front parts of the legs, which trail behind.

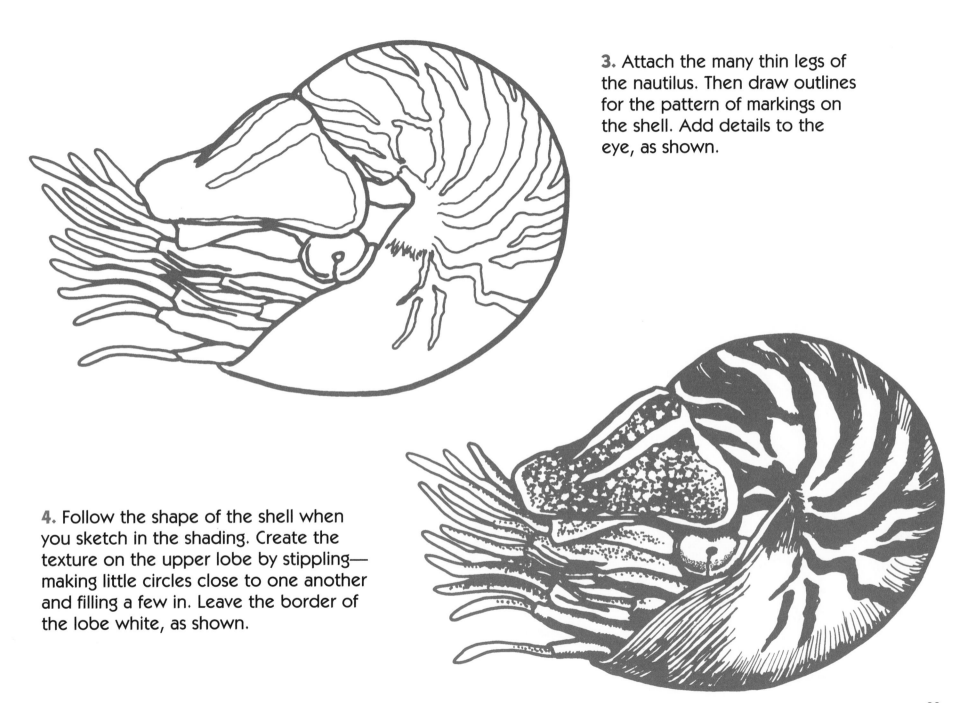

3. Attach the many thin legs of the nautilus. Then draw outlines for the pattern of markings on the shell. Add details to the eye, as shown.

4. Follow the shape of the shell when you sketch in the shading. Create the texture on the upper lobe by stippling— making little circles close to one another and filling a few in. Leave the border of the lobe white, as shown.

Reef Scene

Imagine yourself at a warm, colorful, tropical coral reef surrounded by coral boulders, purple and green sea fans, red and orange sponges dotting the rock, and bright yellow tube sponges. Use your imagination—and your drawing skills—to create various underwater scenes. The background shown here is only one of endless possibilities. When you create your own, add as many different sea creatures as you like.

Tip: Don't just draw in the space around the objects. Draw over, between, and behind them. Perhaps just the front half of a shark is visible behind the boat, or a small fish is lurking between the sea fans. Use your imagination and, most of all, have fun!

Index

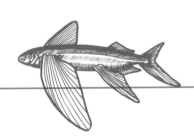
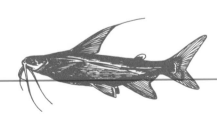

Great Barracuda
pages 10-11

Great Hammerhead Shark
pages 50-51

Great White Shark
pages 34-35

Hatchetfish
pages 40-41

Hawksbill Sea Turtle
pages 36-37

Hermit Crab
pages 52-53

Horn Shark
pages 86-87

Horseshoe Crab
pages 42-43

Lesser Electric Ray
page 7

Manatee
pages 32-33

Manta Ray
page 80

Mola-mola
page 81

Moray Eel
pages 46-47

Nautilus
pages 88-89

Octopus
pages 54-55

Orca
pages 8-9

Pacific Sockeye Salmon
pages 74-75

Peacock Flounder
pages 22-23

Porcupine Fish
pages 58-59

Portuguese Man-o'-war
pages 72-73

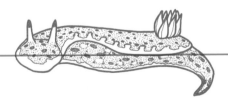

Purple-spotted Sea Goddess
pages 48-49

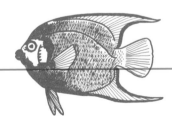

Queen Angelfish
pages 12-13

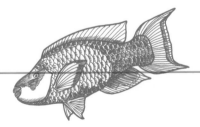

Rainbow Parrotfish
pages 56-57

Reef Scene
pages 90-91

Sargassum Triggerfish
pages 82-83

Sea Horse
pages 60-61

Southern Stingray
pages 76-77

Sperm Whale
pages 62-63

Tiger Grouper
pages 38-39

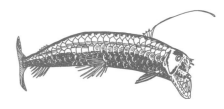

Viperfish
pages 68-69

Walrus
pages 84-85

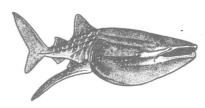

Whale Shark
pages 70-71

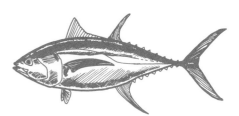

Yellowfin Tuna
pages 66-67